RESTORING
Your Beautiful Life

ENDORSEMENTS

Restoring Your Beautiful Life is a soul stirring compilation of insightful reflections; reflections that contain the wisdom of a well examined life, and that can stimulate you to have your own reflections, arriving at your own unique insights. Whether you read a few pages at a time, or the whole book in one setting (a more likely scenario) you will be touched by the women who have made this book what it is!

~ Dr. Clare Albright
    Author of *Neurofeedback: Transforming Your Life with Brain Biofeedback*
    www.DrClarity.com

~

The courage of these women to share their stories is healing for all of us. Their journeys are a beacon for all who know the *'dark night of the soul'* and look for inspiration to turn their lives around.

~ Jim Morningstar, Ph.D.
    Director, Transformations Incorporated

~

Everyone has a story. The women in *Restoring Your Beautiful Life* not only share their stories, but they also share how they changed from victim mentality to creating the life they truly desire. Being willing to look for and answer the tough questions that were keeping them stuck shows great courage. They are an inspiration to me, and I know they will encourage you as well.

~ Cindy Ray
    Author, *Beyond Beautiful*, Lifecoach, Certified Parenting Educator

~

A truly and deeply inspiring read, reminding us that even in our darkest moments to let go and allow grace, love, truth, forgiveness, the Divine and gratitude to guide us in life and see how miracles then take over our life!

~ Shelyn Somani, M.D.
    Physician, Acupuncturist & Primordial Sound Meditation Instructor

~

These true stories of regular people overcoming difficult times demonstrate that we all have the power to heal ourselves, forgive even the most egregious behavior, and move into creating the life we were meant to live.

~ Kathryn Reeves, Psy.D., Take Charge! Spiritual Coach
    Author, *Take Charge! A Pocket Guide for Coping with Life*
    Radio Show Host – KAHI Radio AM950

I am humbled. These strong women have bravely bared their complicated, often tragic stories to show us that life, beautiful life, can and does go on. As you cry with them through tales of abuse, neglect and self-loathing, and sometimes laugh at the absurdity of it all, you can't help but feel a growing strength and power unfold as you watch each of their lives gain light through the tools they have acquired and mastered: Perspective. Gratitude. Accountabiiity. Confidence ... and, ultimately, Self-Love.

As a parent and an advocate in the adoption community, these are useful tools for many of us who have struggled with infertility and not understood at the time, why we were being put through the paces. As each of my children was placed in my arms, my reasons became apparent – these were the children meant to be in my life .. the ones meant to call me "Mommy." I hope to share this book with folks that are now going through the same struggles – I know that they can draw strength and light as they become witness to the tales of these incredible women.

~ Shila M. Khan
  Education/Conference Chair and former President
  Chicago Area Families for Adoption – www.caffa.org

~

As you read each author's journey in *Restoring Your Beautiful Life*, you will feel as if you are talking with special friends. The insight, wisdom and personal struggles to find their own personal power and happiness will truly inspire you. Each story lets you know you are not alone and that you have the inner strength and wisdom to achieve the life you desire.

~ Robyn Podboy, Co-Author of *Beyond Beautiful*, Speaker, Facilitator to
  Pathway Retreats, Heal Your Life® licensed workshop leader/teacher.
  robynpodboy@aol.com
  http://shineyourlightnow.com

~

What you hold in your hands is more than just a book! It is a guide that will free your spirit by helping you unlock that beautiful soul you were born as. Through life's ups and downs, we often lose that magnificence and radiance we are born with. Allow the stories in this book to awaken that part of you as you share in the deep and powerful transformation of these amazing individuals just like you and me, that have face some insurmountable odds, disappointments and set-backs, but yet channeled those into power and triumph by working through and healing their inner spirit. May these stories uplift you into your own spiritual breakthrough, expansion and returning to that beautiful soul within.

~ Nachhi Randhawa, Transformational Money & Business
  Breakthrough Coach
  www.GrandLifeSolutions.com

" *There are times I ask myself,*

Am I LOOKING for

what's GOOD or am I

LOOKING

for what ISN'T **? "**

I notice when I am LOOKING

more often for what's

GOOD – LIFE IS GOOD.

When I am LOOKING for what ISN'T

– well, life ISN'T AS good. When I am

AWARE that I am not looking for "good" –

I can CHOOSE to CHANGE my FOCUS ...

and be filled with Infinite Blessings.

~Lisa Hardwick

RESTORING
Your Beautiful Life

ISBN: 978-0-9818791-7-8

BECKWORTH PUBLICATIONS

3108 E 10th St ~ Trenton, Mo 64683 ~ 660-204-4088

Ordering information: Quantity Sales. Special discounts are available on quantity purchases
by corporations, associations, and others. For details, contact the "Special Sales Department at
Beckworth Publications."

Beckworth Publications and the Beckworth Publications logo are trademarks of Beckworth
Publications.

Printed in the United States of America.

Library of Congress Cataloging-in-Publication Data.

Hardwick, Lisa
Restoring Your Beautiful Life: True Stories of Extraordinary Courage, Hope, Healing and Love

Library of Congress Control Number: 2011909351

Cover and Interior Graphic Design: Mike Baugher
Senior Editor: Jack Hopkins
Associate Editor: Nancy Newman
Compiled by: Lisa A. Hardwick
Photographers: Kaitlin Lampley, Kent Henderson, Joe Mandeville, David Vernon, Angie
Nemanic, Chak Koonapareddy, Karen Hoyle, Ramsay & Winsor Photography, Jim Kratz

CONTENTS

FOREWORD

When we are born unto this earth – we are beautiful. Every part of our being and soul is beautiful. As we grow, we are introduced to many aspects throughout our evolvement which leave scars on our soul and pain in our heart. Our subconscious becomes conditioned with that which is both positive and negative. The negative conditioning makes living beautifully more difficult, more challenging than many are willing to admit. The "fear" seems to take over and the result is a life which appears to be anything but beautiful. Our lives are filled with anger, resentment, blame and results in depression, addiction, severe anxiety, diseases and hopelessness.

When we realize our life seems to be extremely off balance, it's challenging to know who to discuss the uneasiness with and how. Perhaps you are afraid because the cloud of depression is moving in more rapidly than the last episode or your relationships seem to be more challenging or perhaps you are worried about your finances. When feelings of fear about such things arise, it may feel odd to mention it during your regular meeting with the girls at Starbucks on Saturday morning. Wouldn't you agree? Many times, we just "don't discuss" such matters.

We go throughout our day coping with all of the overwhelming tasks, responsibilities and suppressed thoughts while wearing that heavy mask that says "Everything is fine! I'm fine! Are you fine? Oh, I'm sure we are all fine!" This is how we treat each other, this is how we are subconsciously conditioning the next generation, this is how we walk around in a fog as we think everyone else has life figured out and we don't - all due to our own conditioning and limited communication.

During our journey many of us begin to understand that our past challenges and pain were indeed a beautiful gift. A gift that led us to back to the beautiful being we were created to be. We realize this when we "step out" to another to share those stories of past challenges and we find we are in the company of others who have experienced the same. Perhaps not the exact same story, however the exact same "awakening" to their own beautiful new self.

Why did it take so long for us to take that leap to share our truths so we could experience this feeling of unity and love? Many may agree that all things come in its perfect timing. Perhaps your perfect timing may be presented to you while reading one of the magnificent stories within this book you are presently holding in your hands.

All of the stories derive from a diversified group of women who experienced different lives and different circumstances that led to a beautiful awakening to their own Truth. Their story may be my story…or your story…. yet all in all each story is "our" story. For when our sisters heal and become whole, they take us by the hand to lead us to our own individual truths, and we become healthy and whole as well. The more who speak their truth, the more lives are affected with the beautiful light of healing and love.

The caring and compassionate women you will meet within these pages share their human spirit through raw words with a frankly speaking mentality. Words of realness that our soul longs for each and every day of our existence on this planet. They are now able to shine their light due to the removal of the dark heavy masks that they each wore for many years. They are free and they want this gift of freedom to be presented to you. For if individuals speak their truth, others will be more open to do so as well. These women have stepped into their power and have healed their soul from past pain, and they have reclaimed their beauty. Now that pain from their past is simply "just a story" and no longer rears its destructiveness in their lives.

These women have restored their lives through transforming their circumstances and now each live the extraordinary personal lives they know they were created to live. May their heartfelt sharing assist with finding yourself happy, healthy and whole.

~ Lisa A. Hardwick
Author of From Broken To Beautiful
www.lisahardwick.com

INTRODUCTION
by Nancy Newman

What challenges and obstacles have you encountered in your life? Have there been times that you've felt "broken," or like you're just about to break open? You may even be feeling that way at this very moment. You may believe that what you have experienced is unique; that no one else could possibly understand, or that no one else has ever gone through it. It is true that no one has had your EXACT experience, because we each come with our own history; however, chances are that you will find yourself and similar feelings and experiences in the story of one or more of the women in this book. In these stories, you will be able to see that there IS hope: Hope for an end to the pain, hope for a new beginning … hope to restore the beautiful life that each of us are entitled to live!

MELISSA J. WHITE had what many would believe was that beautiful life. At 32, she was an attorney with her own private practice. She was married to her best friend – who also happened to be a doctor. For the first time in her life, she wasn't worried about money. But instead of being happy living what she thought should be the beautiful life, she was miserable. Somewhere deep in her being, she felt she was living behind a mask, living – not the beautiful life – but a life that was a fraud. But why?

The more she tried to make sense of it intellectually, the more the answers to basic questions eluded her: "Who was I? And how had I gotten here? I thought I did everything right. But if I did do everything right, why wasn't I happy? Who lied to me along the way? Who created this mask, and how could I pry it off? How could I find my way home…back to myself, to my truth? "

Melissa found her answers in writing, trusting that in the silence of the pages, she would find the voice that had eluded her for so long. Accompany Melissa on her journey to find her way back to herself, to her beautiful life.

TERRY VOLIN REAM got up one night on what she thought was going to be a routine visit to the bathroom, but on the way discovered she was dragging her left side. No matter how she tried to rationalize the symptoms and the fear away, she realized she was having a stroke. The doctors at the hospital confirmed her fears – she had suffered a stroke that had paralyzed her left side.

Her next three months involved leaving for rehab every morning at 6:00 a.m., returning home that night at 6:00 p.m. exhausted, going to sleep, then starting over again the next morning. She had been told that if she were able to recover enough to go back to work, it would be at least a year – IF she was able to return to work at all!

Terry was fortunate to have the loving support of her family and friends, and to discover the principles of the mind-body-spirit connection as taught by Louise L. Hay in the book, *You Can Heal Your Life*. She immediately began to visualize herself as healthy and whole, and amazed everyone around her when she was able to make a miraculous recovery in far less time than the doctors imagined could be possible and to a far greater degree than anyone thought possible – except for Terry!

Even though she made an almost total recovery, the doctors had never been able to find a physical cause for the stroke. But Terry knew that the real reason had to be beyond the physical so she began to take a look at her life and found the causes. Terry's story will show you that there is always hope, and there is always a way to restore your beautiful life if you're willing to do the mental work.

Terry and her story are an inspiration for us all.

TAMMY GYNELL LAGOSKI grew up in a small rural setting in Illinois and experienced a childhood filled with low self-esteem, mixed signals, secrets (alcoholism and physical abuse) and a broken family.

The physical abuse was not just toward Tammy, but extended to her mother and her brothers. It was a confusing time because interspersed with her step-father's violent alcoholic rages and criticism , there would be really fun family times. By the time she was a teenager, she lived in fear of being rejected because of her looks, lack of smarts, or education, or not being sophisticated enough to blend in with a new community and fear of not succeeding in college. She experienced unemployment, divorce, several moves, illness, severe depression and a suicide attempt. Her life was anything but the beautiful life she was meant to live.

For Tammy, it was finding her faith in God that guided her, shielded her and protected her when life seemed bleak and colorless. Although at times her faith left her, she found her way back to herself and to God.

Tammy encourages each person to let yourself shine, and to allow yourself to be free of the past, the anger and the low self-esteem. She asks us to consider the Kaleidoscope of life: Will the scope remain stuck in the dark abyss of life's ugliness or will the scope turn and reveal the beauty of life, and the peace that God has in store for you?

Tammy chose to turn the scope and accept the beauty of self, and the Holy Spirit.

MOLLY WELESKI didn't always have the beautiful life she experiences today and, as a result, awakens every morning with a sense of gratitude. She begins each day by taking time to thank God for her many blessings and gifts. She feels that her life is a testament to the thought that some of God's greatest gifts are unanswered prayers. Though her lessons have been painful, through the love she has received from her family, she has come to the beautiful life she now has.

Molly grew up impoverished in Canada as the seventh of eight children in a family full of shame. There was criticism and judgment from the community that the parents had more children than they could care for, and were, therefore, not "a morally fit family." In addition, there was physical, sexual and emotional abuse. There was no trust in their household, and her home life was quite unpredictable most of the time.

All her life, Molly wanted to be a mother – a better mother than she felt she had had. She was initially plagued with infertility problems but eventually gave birth to a healthy baby boy. After that she endured a miscarriage and a pregnancy that had to be terminated because of rare complications with the fetus. And, then, finally, the birth of a healthy baby girl. But her desire to be a good mother was compromised by depression and insecurities.

Join Molly as she tells her story of overcoming her childhood, her depression and insecurities to claim the beautiful life she longed to have.

KIMBERLY S. PRATTE came to her beautiful life through self-awareness and healing through forgiveness. She tells how her "paradigm shift" was only possible because she was able to visualize it, understand it, and was determined to reach it and completely remember it, which ultimately led to a sense of well-being, a state of wellness in every aspect of her life unlike anything she had ever experienced before.

Kimberly tells us how life had beaten her down to a point where she truly believed that no one would ever really love her. She felt that "she" didn't matter, and always made sure that everyone else's needs were met and they were happy. She felt frozen in a reality of creating negative energy within and around herself. She seemed to always attract abuse and abusive relationships.

She feels her pattern started when her father left the family when Kimberly was only 2-1/2 years old. Eventually her mother had to leave the children with the grandparents so she could work, and she only saw her children on the weekends. It was the birth of another younger brother and the suicide of her beloved grandfather that really shattered her world, leaving her feeling alone, betrayed and abandoned.

Kimberly was able to turn her life around when she found Jim Morningstar and Transformations USA and the School of Integrative Psychology in Milwaukee, Wisconsin. Through this work, she has gone through a long journey of self-discovery and reconnecting with herself to get back to the truth of who she really is.

Kimberly takes us through the steps to finding and knowing your truth, and living your beautiful life.

SHELLY YORK will share with you the tumultuous period during which she experienced the deaths of several family members, including the suicide of her dad's father. During this same period of time, she suffered a miscarriage and went through severe financial struggles resulting in bankruptcy. Shortly after that, her cherished father died in his sleep during a nap.

She feels that she was at a turning point in her life. She had recently lost her dad, quit a job that she hated, had moved back in with her mother (so her mother wouldn't be alone), and was stuck in an unhappy and loveless marriage. She felt that there just had to be more to life. At that point, she watched the DVD by Louise L. Hay called *You Can Heal Your Life*, then immediately went out and bought the book of the same name.

Shelly's life began to change at that moment. She still had some painful lessons to go through, but through it all, learned that she was deserving of love. She discovered that through honesty and authenticity she received the gift of unconditional love.

Shelly went through seven painful years of struggle and grief to ultimately find her way to her authentic self, and to find her beautiful life.

JODY KRATZ believes that major life changes must start from within, that your outer world cannot change until you work to change your inner world.

She will lead us through her younger years as the daughter of an alcoholic father who suffered from depression. Her beloved older brother committed suicide which set Jody into a cycle of depression, panic attacks, an abortion, guilt, severe illness and drinking. After she married and had kids, she realized that her husband was also an alcoholic.

Although her husband could be a great father to her kids, his mental illnesses, drinking, secretive behaviors and ultimately losing his company really set him into a tailspin which resulted in his eventual suicide.

As a nurse and working a long distance from her home, she would pass the long hours in the car listening to tapes such as a *Course in Miracles* and *The Power of Now* by Eckhart Tolle which would ultimately change her life. Jody takes us through her turbulent and chaotic life then teaches us the basics of how she turned her life around.

Jody is currently building a holistic business and believes she is now doing what she was meant to do in this life time. She tells us that she is loving every second of her beautifully restored new life!

CAROL ROESE was born in Brazil as the youngest of four children. She feels that her childhood was great, but it was when she was about 18 years old that she began to live with manipulation, jealousy and disagreements, and soon desperation and depression were a part of her life. She was introduced to the concept of creating your life with your thoughts by a psychologist in Brazil and that's when her life began to change.

She moved to the United States totally on faith, with no friends, no job and not knowing where she wanted to live. She first lived in San Diego, then later moved to Miami where she felt the culture and the people were more like Brazil. Again, she had no job, no friends but trusted her inner voice that Miami was the place for her to be.

In San Diego Carol had read many Louise Hay books and really began to embrace and use the philosophies, eventually becoming a licensed Heal Your Life ® Teacher and Workshop leader, which is based on the teachings and philosophies of Louise Hay.

Carol tells us that she doesn't know what she will be doing next in life, but she does know that she can change her reality and her experiences anytime she wants. She will teach you how to use affirmations and positive thoughts by explaining how she has created her wonderful, beautiful life in America!

In the stories of these eight women, you will find abuse, grief, loss, depression, suicide, alcoholism, broken families, poverty and a myriad of other conditions with which almost anyone can identify. But more importantly, you will also find love, perseverance, tenacity, endurance, courage, dignity, passion, and self-respect. In their journeys, they have found ways to transcend their life circumstances and restore their beautiful lives. And so can you!

MELISSA J. WHITE

Chapter 1:
A Life Worth Living

CHAPTER 1
A Life Worth Living

" Solitude can be a much-to-be-desired condition.
Not only is it acceptable to be alone,
at times it is positively to be wished for.
In silence, we listen to ourselves, and in the quietude,
we may even hear the voice of God. **"**
~ Maya Angelou

For as long as I can remember, I've been trying to hear that voice…trying to discover my purpose. But the answers seemed to elude me. Where was God, and why couldn't I hear Him?

I grew up in the church – United Methodist to be exact. I was taught that God was a man…that God was judgmental…that God was separate. So I kept listening for the answers God had for me. What was my purpose? What was the "right" thing to do?

I looked for the answers in the ways I was taught to look for them. I looked outside myself. I looked to the church. I looked to society. I questioned my teachers, listened to friends, and acquiesced to family. But I didn't listen to myself very much. What did I know? And what would others think if what I thought I knew went against everything they thought was "right" and "good" and "safe"?

I was the kind of kid that always did the "right" thing. I was an overachiever. I set goals, and I reached them. So it didn't take me long to get the hang of climbing the ladder and racking up the accomplishments. I told myself that "after I finish _____, then I'll be happy. Then I'll live." But that day never came. And as I approached my 30s, I knew that somehow that approach – the societal way of achieving – did not work for me.

At 32, I had, by many societal standards, "made it." I was an attorney with my own private practice. I was married to my best friend – who also happened to be a doctor. For the first time in my life, I really didn't have to worry about money. By many standards, I should have been happy. But I was absolutely miserable. The more I tried to make sense of it intellectually, the more the answers eluded me.

Perhaps I should have a child, some would say. But somehow I knew that I had nothing to offer a child. Somewhere deep within my being I felt that my life was a fraud. That I had been living behind a mask.

Who was I? And how had I gotten here? I thought I did everything right. But if I did do everything right, why wasn't I happy? Who lied to me along the way? Who created this mask, and how could I pry it off? How could I find my way home...back to myself, to my truth?

These are some of the questions that I asked as I began to write, trusting that in the silence of the pages, I would find the voice that had eluded me for so long.

SUCCESS

A goal to reach
A destination found
All is well within reach
My life is spinning round.

Not a moment to spare
Not a second to ponder
All the while
My thoughts wander.

How could life's path
Send me astray
While the success I yearn
Remains at bay?

Maybe success
Is not defined
By awards or money
Or devotion to mankind.

Maybe success
Lies in being true
To the self deep within
Both me and you.

~Melissa J. White

I wrote this poem years ago before I had any idea what it meant. In my late 20s at the time, I was struggling to figure out why my "success" wasn't making me happy. Finally, after setting the poem aside for several days or weeks, it just came to me. I did not fully comprehend, at that time, that this poem held the answer to the question that had eluded me for so long.

Not only did it hold the answer, but I received the answer in kind – from deep within my being. Some may call it the God within. Others might say it's intuition. And some might call it the inner self. Regardless of the terminology, the goal is the same – to be true to yourself. While "be true to yourself" has become a mantra for our generation, how is this achieved?

Society is premised upon the concept that in order to succeed, you must adhere to a set of rules –be it etiquette, organizational structure, religion, the legal system, the medical and psychiatric communities, the "ladder of success," etc. However, if we take this premise to its extreme, we can see how this premise can destruct, rather than help. From a sociological viewpoint, rules are no longer keeping society intact.

All kinds of people make rules and many follow them. But who is making the rules and under what authority? The "rules" of the playground, in some communities, tell kids that it's okay to sell drugs and carry guns. Some religions, in their most radical form, tell their followers that it's okay to kill innocent people in the name of religion. Likewise, "crooked" and "politicians" have been linked together enough to make many wonder about the ethics of our government.

The point is this: Which rules do you follow? While it may seem common sense to some of us that not killing others is a rule we should not break, it may not be so clear to others. In an environment that does not value individual expression, but rather, encourages rule-following and group think, breaking away from outside influence may not even be a consideration. Moreover, in certain circumstances, such as war, killing is viewed as an accepted and necessary practice. In short, if we are constantly looking outside ourselves for the "right" answer, how will we hear our inner wisdom when we journey down the "wrong" path? Until we learn to listen to our innate wisdom, we, as a society, will continue to work against each other, rather than with each other.

The societal rule-centeredness also has another inherent flaw. Because rule-following does not encourage independent action, obedience to rules does not encourage people to take responsibility for their actions. There are all kinds of rules and all kinds of interpretations on how those rules should be followed, making "rule-breaking," on some level, an everyday occurrence. This "rule-breaking" leaves those seemingly afflicted by the broken rules as "victims." The "victim" is then pitied and the "perpetrator" persecuted. This victim mentality is perpetuated throughout our society from our legal system to our psychiatric community. But the line between victim and perpetrator is not always clear. As we have seen all too often, "perpetrators" themselves were once "victims."

It is a vicious cycle born of fear. Fear that causes people to feel they need rules to protect them. Fear that causes people to follow rules. Fear that causes people to fear being victimized. Fear that causes people to blame others for their predicament. The stronger the fear, the stronger the perceived need to control, blame, or victimize. And the cycle continues.

We, as a society, are so focused on following rules and placing blame that we seldom listen to our own voices. If we, as individuals, are not true to ourselves, how can we ever be true to anyone else? Perhaps instead of focusing on rules, we should each be more focused on following that inner knowing within each of us.

> **66** We do not see things the way they are,
>
> we see things as we are. **99**
>
> *~Anais Nin*

I used to believe that my purpose was to take care of others. First, I went into counseling, hoping to help others. But I felt it was too reactive. So I became a lawyer, thinking it would be more proactive. I was wrong. Both, in my experience, were victim-oriented. Neither encouraged the "victim" to take any responsibility.

And they are both other-centered. Let's face it. We go to a counselor to get help with our "problems." We employ a lawyer to fight against our "problems." These fields – as others – are guided by a set of "rules." These "rules" are established by others to better understand, explain, or control people, situations, and behaviors. But why the need to control? Fear. Plain and simple. When people fear something or someone, they tend to create a framework in which to understand it and/or control it in order to feel that they have control of their lives. They do this because they want to feel less afraid.

But does it really work? Are we any less afraid? I think it's quite the contrary.

Let's look at prejudice, for example. While prejudice is learned, it has, at its core, fear. When someone has what they consider a negative experience with someone else, fear sets in. The person who had the negative experience makes a mental note that people with certain physical, mental or other characteristics act a certain way and, therefore, should be treated a certain way. The more this experience occurs, the stronger the prejudice. Or, in other words, the stronger the fear.

The result, of course, is that when the person who had the negative experience meets someone who has the same physical, mental or other characteristics, she reacts from that fear. The unsuspecting other person then has a "negative" experience and begins to also create prejudices based upon fear. And the cycle continues. Fear turns into hate and/or anger. One person tells the next person and the cycle accelerates. Love never enters the equation.

But my prejudices are based on truths, you say. Okay, whose truths are they based on? Do you really know enough about the other person to know the truth?

Let's consider this scenario: You are driving along the beltway in rush hour traffic when a red-headed teenager, driving a black Porsche 911 begins darting in and out of traffic, cutting you off and nearly causing several wrecks. She seems to ignore the traffic around her and finally gets off at a nearby exit, just missing a passing cop.

You think one or any of the following: Rich brat. Teenagers are irresponsible and inconsiderate. Red heads are fiery. Girls shouldn't be allowed to drive. No good cops – they're never there when you need them. Little did you know that the red-headed teenager had been babysitting for her doctor's son when he fell and hit his head on the coffee table. He had a wide gash over his eye which was bleeding profusely. When the teenager called to inform the doctor of the situation, the doctor told her to bring the boy to the hospital where she was working and would be waiting for him. The teenager did not have a car, so the doctor told her to use her extra car, a Porsche 911. The teenager was not used to driving in rush hour traffic and did not know what she was getting into. The boy was losing blood and the teenager became concerned for his survival, so she did her best to get through the traffic and get the boy to the hospital.

The truth is that we will never fully understand another person's perspective. Even siblings brought up in the same family bring different personalities and overall experiences to the table. The best we can do is attempt to see things from another person's point of view. Still, we never know all that comprises their particular view and experience of the world. The best we can do is step out in love and compassion, recognizing that no two people see the world exactly the same way. No two people have the same personality, experiences, or fears. If we focus on our own capacity to love, instead of fear, we can begin to see that love – or the cry for love – exists all around us.

> **66** I must not fear. Fear is the mind-killer
>
> Fear is the little-death that brings total obliteration
>
> I will face my fear. I will permit it to pass over me and through me.
>
> And when it has gone past I will turn the inner eye to see its path.
>
> Where the fear has gone there will be nothing.
>
> Only I will remain. **99**
>
> ~ *Frank Herbert*

So how do we act from love instead of fear? Perhaps we should first look at fear and actions purportedly taken in the name of love or as a cry for love.[1]

ANN AND BRIAN

Ann and Brian met after a period of heartache on both parts. He was everything she ever wanted and more. Their love grew fast and deep. The connection they felt was indescribable. They each were convinced that they were meant to be together forever.

As time went on, Brian started to become possessive and controlling. Ann tried to fix the problem by either pacifying him or doing whatever she wanted to do regardless of what Brian said, thinking it was a phase that he was going through. But that just made Brian act out even more.

Growing up, Brian found that the people he loved always left him and/or were never there for him – though he never would have admitted this (he was a very independent man). From the beginning, he was afraid of losing Ann, just as he had all his other loved ones, so he held onto her as tightly as he could.

Ann had grown up believing that other people come first – always giving love, but never receiving it in the way she would have liked. She was afraid of losing the love she knew she had found, so Ann waited, all the time trying to "fix" Brian.

Ann and Brian are both crying for love and acting out of fear. Ann is putting Brian's insecurities before her own needs because she believes that love means other people come first. Brian is smothering Ann with his love out of the fear that she will abandon him just as everyone else has. Brian does not realize that this "love" is consumed by fear and that that fear, combined with Ann's fear, is destroying the relationship. They claim they are in love, but they really are in fear.

SHEILA AND NANCY

Sheila was four years old when Nancy was born. She was very excited about the new addition to her family and proudly helped to take care of her little sister. As children, Nancy looked up to Sheila, who was always there when she needed her.

As they got older, Nancy and Sheila developed their own interests and pursuits – born, perhaps, out of sibling rivalry. As adults, the differences between Sheila and Nancy grew. Both longed for a sisterly relationship but the distance between them seemed more and more impossible to bridge.

Sheila did not understand the decisions that Nancy was making, which seemed, to her, unconventional and adverse to anything she felt she knew about Nancy. Therefore, Sheila tried everything she could to coerce Nancy into submitting to her idea of who Nancy should be.

Nancy, feeling persecuted by her sister, began to withdraw from the relationship. Over the years, she had teetered between having ferocious fights with her sister and acquiescing to her. She had always felt misunderstood by her and often tried, to no avail, to explain herself to Sheila.

Sheila claims that her attempts to reel her sister back are based in love, but they are really based in fear. Likewise, Nancy feels so persecuted and misunderstood that she has grown to fear being around her sister. Both sisters are hurt and are looking for someone to blame. Sheila can't understand her sister's behavior and blames her for walking away from the relationship. Nancy blames her sister for not supporting her decisions and pushing her away. The fear that has overtaken their mutual relationship began as a cry for love.

Both Sheila and Nancy and Ann and Brian are looking outside of themselves for love. They do this based upon the societal belief that love is something that we obtain from others. Do these scenarios sound familiar? Collectively, we enter into this dance we call love – be it romantic or platonic – most of the time, stepping out in fear instead of love. We let fear lead and, in doing so, we deny ourselves – and, ultimately, each other, of love.

66 To thine own self be true,

and it must follow,

as the night the day,

thou canst not then be false to any man. **99**

~ William Shakespeare

While many of us know the first line of this quote from Shakespeare, the lines that follow may not be as familiar. This quote, taken from "Hamlet," is the final piece of advice given by Polonius to his son. He is counseling him to take care of himself first.

To many of us, this may seem backwards. We, as a society, are often taught, directly or indirectly, that love means putting others first. Because this caretaking is so highly valued, some of us get very good at taking care of others. We even denote "roles" to people so that they know what their duties are within a given relationship.

We sometimes work so hard at these duties that we have little time for ourselves. Ultimately, we suffer. We get sick. We are exhausted. We become resentful. We are running on fumes. Then, we are no help to anyone.

This is why when you board an airplane that the flight attendant advises you that if you are traveling with someone who needs assistance to put the oxygen mask on yourself first. If you do not take care of yourself first, you cannot help anyone else. This is not just helpful advice to use in an emergency. It is not "selfishness" – at least not in the way our society normally views selfishness. It is self love which is at the core of each of us.

If we access the love within ourselves, we will find that it emanates to all others in our lives. The more we focus on that love within, the more the fear begins to dissolve. What then, is love?

66 Love is patient, love is kind.

It does not envy, it does not boast, it is not proud.

It is not rude, it is not self-seeking,

it is not easily angered, it keeps no record of wrongs.

Love does not delight in evil but rejoices in the truth.

It always protects, always trusts, always hopes, always perseveres.

Love never fails…. **99**

~ I Corinthians 13:4-8.

Though many of us, regardless of religious background, would tend to agree with this definition, at least in part, how many of us can say that we truly love like this? There are certain individuals we find easy to love, but what about those who are challenging to love? Do we find ourselves keeping a record of wrongs? Are we secretly happy when something "bad" happens to them? Do we judge people as either "good" or "bad," depending upon the actions they take or the reputation they have created?

If we are successful in loving even the most challenging of people, do we stand up for them when they are wrongfully accused? Do we believe the rumors we hear and avoid contact with some people out of fear that the rumors may be right? Despite even the sincerest efforts to genuinely love, do we allow our fears to get the best of us?

How many of us truly have the courage to act out of love, rather than fear? How many of us truly live our lives? Sure, we get up in the morning; we go to work; we get married; we have families; we go on vacations, live for weekends…we do what we are expected to do. But are we truly living our lives or are we living someone else's version of who we should be? Are we too afraid to buck the system, too afraid of being the oddball, too afraid of playing the fool, of being "crazy"?

In her book, *The Myth of Sanity* (pp. 6-8), Martha Stout says:

> [W]e do not choose to die, or to live; we go on surviving. We do not choose nonexistence, nor do we choose complete awareness. We slog on, in a kind of foggy cognitive middle land we call sane, a place where we almost never acknowledge the haze.
>
> Over the years, what my trauma patients have taught me is that this compromise with reality and its traumas is simply not sanity at all. It is a form of madness, and it befuddles our existence. We lose parts of our thoughts in the present, we sabotage the closeness and comfort in our relationships, and we misplace important pieces of ourselves.

> ✲✲✲
>
> Mysteriously, and before we realize what is happening, our lives are transfigured from places of imagination and hope into to-do lists, into day after day of just getting through it. Often we are able to envision only a long road of exhausting hurdles, that leads somewhere we are no longer at all certain we even want to go. Instead of having dreams we merely protect ourselves. We expend our brief and precious life force in the practice of damage control.

Protection of selves. Damage control. Fear.

Are we as a society so concerned with protecting ourselves, following the rules, and reacting to our circumstances that we have forgotten the love that exists in all of us? Are we so afraid of living that we merely survive? Have we become so reliant on meeting societal expectations and getting our own needs met from outside of ourselves that we have lost touch with our own individual selves?

> **❝** At the center of your being you have
>
> The answer;
>
> You know who you are and you know
>
> What you want. **❞**
>
> ~ *Lao-tzu*

All my life, I had been listening to other people. I thought I made my own decisions, but they were still based on someone else's logic, prompting, or approval. I followed the societal view of how to be successful, sent cards on all the right occasions, always did the "right" thing, always took care of others…often to the detriment of myself.

By the time I had reached 33, it was clear to me that the societal view of happiness did not fit for me. I had all the trappings of "success." Yet I was absolutely miserable. What would I do now? And how would I trust that I was going in the right direction?

I knew how to reach goals. As an overachiever, I had gotten good at succeeding at pretty much anything I set out to do. But the rules that I followed didn't work. I was tired, disillusioned and lost. I no longer felt myself around people – as if they somehow would sense that I was a fraud. I had become increasingly withdrawn. I no longer felt I knew myself. Perhaps I never really had.

I had lots of questions but no real answers. Who would I ask anyway? That process, upon which I had relied, had just proven futile. And who could tell me more about myself than me? In the Summer of 2000, I began searching for the answers. Not in a book or from a person. But from within myself.

I took a five-week sabbatical from work which culminated in a 10-day trip to a yoga retreat in the Colorado Rockies. Little did I know, that in the decade that followed, that little retreat would become my sanctuary – my safe haven; my way of finding my way back home. Home to myself.

Restoring Your Beautiful Life

> **❝** When you lose touch with your inner stillness,
>
> you lose touch with yourself.
>
> When you lose touch with yourself,
>
> you lose yourself in the world.
>
> Your innermost sense of self, of who you are,
>
> is inseparable from stillness
>
> This is the I AM that is deeper than form. **❞**
>
> ~ *Eckhart Tolle, Stillness Speaks*

That summer, I slowly started turning more and more of my attention inward. It was difficult to detach from the thoughts that often plagued my mind, but over the years, I have found that the more that I cultivate a climate in which I am able to observe my thoughts and feelings more objectively, the more I have been able to truly listen to my inner wisdom.

For me, I am able to access this inner state through meditation and breath work. I've also found that I can find that meditative state when I'm in nature or engaged in activities such as running, swimming, or yoga. In fact, many, including myself, gravitate to yoga, tai chi, qigong and other mind-body-spirit disciplines because of the deep peace and calm that they are able to cultivate within each process.

I do not believe that the method one uses to access that inner stillness is important. But what I believe is absolutely essential for every one of us is that we access that inner state and that we do so on a daily basis. Daily cultivation of this inner awareness will help us to maintain that inner focus more and more throughout the rest of our day, bringing balance and clarity to each part of our lives.

Moreover, within that state, we will find that all the love we seek from others has been within ourselves all along. We will come to realize that if we do take care of our own inner needs first, our outer world will begin to change in direct reflection. As Polonius advised his son, "it must follow" that an attentive inner life nurtures love, happiness and clarity which can then radiate to the world around us. This concept is not just a poetic notion but is supported in fact.

For instance, in the summer of 1993, a group of scientists measured the effects of meditation on the crime rate in Washington, DC.[2] Approximately 4,000 participants in Transcendental Meditation® and TM-Sidhi® programs gathered to reduce stress and increase coherence in DC. The study showed that crime went down in the District in direct proportion to the number of individuals meditating. Ultimately, a 48% reduction in crime was observed as a direct result of the meditation program. "Given the strength of these results, their consistency with the positive results of previous research, the grave human and financial costs of violent crime, and the lack of other effective and scientific methods to reduce crime, policy makers [were] urged to apply this approach on a large scale for the benefit of society." [3]

Whether or not we are in a position to effect policy, we can each effect change within our own lives. By turning our focus inward on a daily basis, we can more fully and completely live lives full of love, happiness and depth. In doing so, we will find our outer world transformed, as well.

> **66** Two roads diverged in a wood, and I
>
> I took the one less traveled by,
>
> And that has made all the difference. **99**
>
> ~ *Robert Frost*

I wish that I could tell you that the last decade has been easy. It has not. But it has been more and more authentic. As I uncovered each layer of my former self, relationships shifted, jobs changed, homes transitioned. Each new beginning was preceded by a sometimes painful ending. But I am more fully living my life and that, for me, has made all the difference.

I truly have found that whether I have money or not, whether I am in a relationship or not, whether I have a particular career, home or lifestyle is not what makes me happy. For me, it is, unquestionably, an inner state of being, from which that happiness and love emanates. The times in my life when I have been most blissful have been the times when I was most connected to that inner stillness.

At times, other people or situations may have been present, but it was that inner stillness that sustained it all. In fact, I have found that when I'm more fully connected to that inner state, the very outwardly painful events in my life just melt away. And, through that inner connection, I have felt more connected to, and at peace with, the outer world, as well.

This is not to say that I am always in touch with this inner peace. There are days when I keep watching the clock. Often, my thoughts still attempt to get in my way. I'm human. But over time, I find that the cumulative effect of my meditation practice allows me to stay in closer connection to that inner stillness throughout the day more easily. I also have found that the answers to many of my questions arise, without effort, simply because of that connection. My meditation practice is like a relationship; the more I practice, the deeper the connection to that inner state grows.

For me, the road less traveled has been navigated by my inner compass. At times, it has felt like an exercise in trial and error. But I have learned that there really are no mistakes in life. Everything does truly happen for a reason. I have been humbled, time and again, by the support that has always been available to me at just the times when I've needed it, without any effort on my part. Through it all, I have found that the answers that I sought were always there; I just wasn't always listening.

> **"** Let your mind start a journey thru a strange new world.
>
> Leave all thoughts of the world you knew before.
>
> Let your soul take you where you long to be…
>
> Close your eyes, let your spirit start to soar,
>
> and you'll live as you've never lived before. **"**
>
> ~ *Erich Fromm*

Over the years, there have been those who applauded the risks that I took and the decisions that I made, as well as those who thought that I was nuts. But, for me, my natural inquisitiveness and my desire for authenticity were insatiable. And I would not have had it any other way. Crazy or not, I have found that the inner journey is creating, for me, a life worth living.

It is my hope that, in sharing my story, you will find within it some of your own truths and, perhaps, some inspiration for your own journey. The answers that you seek are within you, waiting to be heard.

---

[1] The names and circumstances are hypothetical and for illustrative purposes only.

[2] Institute of Science, Technology and Public Policy.

[3] Reference: Hagelin, J.S., Rainforth, M.V., Orme-Johnson, D.W., Cavanaugh, K. L., Alexander, C.N., Shatkin, S.F., Davies, J.L, Hughes, A.O, and Ross, E. 1999. Effects of group practice of the Transcendental Meditation program on preventing violent crime in Washington D.C.: Results of the National Demonstration Project, June-July, 1993. Social Indicators Research, 47(2): 153-201.

TERRY VOLIN REAM

Chapter 2:
Inspired By A Stroke
A Wake Up Call for Life

CHAPTER 2
Inspired By A Stroke
A Wake Up Call for Life

During the middle of the night, I woke up for my nightly trek to the bathroom. Sleepily I rolled out of bed and slowly made my way to the bathroom when I realized that I was dragging my left foot, and my left arm wasn't working either. My whole left side was slowly becoming inoperable. At first I just wanted to crawl back into bed under the warm covers and pretend it was all a dream. As I tried to climb back into my bed, I realized that I couldn't scoot over to the middle without twisting and turning because my body was not responding to what I wanted it to do.

Clearly, this was not a dream.

I realized that I must be having a stroke. I didn't want to be a cripple. My first thoughts were to go back to sleep and hopefully, make it up to heaven. I had lots of people that I wanted to see up there. When all of a sudden my mind was shouting at me that "I'm not done yet; I still have lots to do…I need more Time!" I squirmed myself back off the bed and woke my son in the other room to tell him to take me to the hospital.

Soon, I found myself connected to many machines and having all different kinds of tests being run on me which was totally terrifying to me; the only test I had ever had outside of school tests was a blood test. To protect myself from the fear of what they might find out, I turned myself inward and observed what was happening to me as if I was watching it happen from the outside looking in. It made it easier to get through the day.

By the next morning, I could hardly talk. My left arm and hand would not move no matter how hard I tried. I was diagnosed with a major stroke that debilitated my entire left side. The stroke had damaged the parts of my brain that controlled my emotions, speech patterns and movement of the left side of my body. My brain could no longer send signals to my nerves to make my body do what I wanted it to do. Sometimes I would laugh uncontrollably and other times I would cry for no reason.

All of the parts on the left side of my body had to be taught how to function again. By relearning how to use all of those parts of my body again, new pathways would be created in my brain. The doctors wanted me to go to the Rehabilitation Institute of Chicago for around the clock in-patient care. The mental part of my brain was still functioning just fine or at least I thought it was and the control-freak inside me just wanted to go home. I didn't want anything to do with in-patient care. The doctors were insisting that it was going to be six months to a year of full-time rehabilitation before I would be well enough to go back to work – adding the caveat of: "If you ever get well-enough to go back to work."   Now, that I look back, I know that I was not being very rational.

There is an out-patient rehabilitation facility which is a branch of the Rehabilitation Institute of Chicago that I agreed would be better for me. This facility had very compassionate and caring therapists. I soon had a Speech Therapist, Occupational Therapist and Physical Therapist assigned to help me get better.   Over the next three months, I left at 6:00 a.m. and returned home at 6:00 p.m. exhausted and ready to crawl into bed. For the next year, I craved sleep. I couldn't wait to get home and climb into bed each night and sleep.

Being handicapped or disabled was not an option for me. I decided I would make myself whole and healthy. About a year prior to having the stroke, my sister had told me about a book by Louise Hay called *You Can Heal Your Life*. I skimmed the book and found it very interesting and even gave copies to some of my friends. I decided at the time that I would use it as a reference book whenever I needed it to resolve any maladies or discomforts. Needless to say, I never thought I would be using it to recover from a stroke.

I clearly needed to use Louise Hay's philosophy to heal myself. I started to write affirmations that I could use within my rehab program. I wrote very simple affirmations that I would be able to remember and repeat in my mind while I was doing my exercises such as:

"I can walk"
"I can lift my arm"
"I can pick up the pieces"
"My fingers move freely"
"I can talk clearly"
"I solve puzzles easily"
"I can control my emotions"

I visualized myself walking freely without a walker and using my arm and hand freely. I had a visualization for every part of myself that I needed to repair. I started watching some of the other people that were in the rehab program with me. They had no hope in their eyes; I knew they had given up. They were going through the motions of doing what the therapist was telling them to do to repair their body but they did not believe it in their mind and in their heart. They were going to complete their rehab program and still not be prepared to go on with their life as a whole and healthy person. I was getting better at an amazing rate of speed. I had to believe that the affirmations I was repeating over and over were helping to make the cellular changes in my body to heal.

A miracle had happened for me. Family and friends had been praying for me. I also used the mind, body, spirit connection to help me to heal my body. Instead of taking a year to rehabilitate; I did it in three months and was released to drive and to go back to work. I am very grateful for the help I received from family, friends, and therapists; they were all integral to my healing.

I had healed my body but I knew that if I didn't fix what had caused the stroke to happen in the first place my body would recreate the stroke in another way. The doctors were able to show me pictures of what the stroke had done to my brain but they were unable to find a cause. They could not find any aneurysms, tumors or problems with my heart. Many times a stroke can be caused by the abnormal blood flow from the heart to the brain but they couldn't find any indication that this had happened. All they could recommend was to continue with the exercises recommended by the therapists in my rehab program. In my heart, I knew that I needed to make changes in my life if I didn't want it to happen again. I reviewed what I was doing prior to having the stroke, a snapshot of my life was:

~ Working full-time as a Business Systems Analyst at a Fortune 100 Company often working 10 - 12 hours a day.

~ My daughter had moved in with me with my three grandchildren, and we had just moved into a house because the town home I was living in was not big enough.

~ We had been in the house about six months, when I realized the utilities were much higher than I anticipated. So, I took a part-time job on the weekends to help cover the extra expenses.

~ Running a Mary Kay Business that also helped to supplement my income.

~ Working on my MBA at Lake Forest Graduate School of Management

~ Spending Saturdays helping my Mom; she lived an hour away and couldn't drive because of macular degeneration. So, I ran her errands and spent time visiting her.

Have you ever heard the term "women who do too much"? I was clearly trying to cram way too much into my life. I had to prioritize and eliminate what was not needed at this time. In addition to eliminating what was not a priority, I also had to figure out what I was telling myself mentally and eliminate that from my life too. This stroke was a huge wake-up call for me!

I decided I needed to de-clutter my mind before I could free-up space to think clearly and focus. I stopped working part-time on the weekends, and we tightened our belts at home so we could make ends meet. I decided I didn't need to have an MBA; my heart wasn't into learning more about business, anyway. By eliminating the things that were not serving a good purpose in my life, I was freeing my mind and spirit to work on where I could make a difference in the world.

For the past 20 years, I had been studying spirituality and metaphysics in some form or another. I read many books and listened to self-help and spiritual CD's. My house was filled with books; I have five floor- to-ceiling book shelves filled with spiritual and metaphysical books. I thought to myself that with all of this knowledge at my fingertips, I should know exactly what I needed to do. However, I had no clue what my next steps should be. I started to pay close attention to my thoughts. I realized that I was using the word "should" a lot. I had a lot of "shoulds" which meant that I had a lot of limiting beliefs that I needed to fix.

Figuring out what I needed to change wasn't easy. I had eliminated some of the extra "noise" in my life but hadn't found the nugget of change that I knew was hiding inside of me that was critical to getting better. I had to slow down and listen to my inner feelings. I knew how to meditate but I didn't meditate consistently. So, that was one of the things I knew I needed to make time to do; I had to allow time to quiet my mind. By quieting my mind, I found new ideas starting to bubble to the surface. I was getting closer to finding my passion. I now know who I am. I figured out why I do some of the things I do.

I remembered riding home from church one day in the station wagon; I was about ten years old. There were eight of us kids in the station wagon picking on each other and causing a ruckus when my Dad asked us if we knew what the sermon was about. None of us could answer him; so, he answered it himself. The sermon was about "Kindness." He said that "Kindness" was one of the most important virtues in life. Interestingly, the next day at school, my teacher asked the same question. I was the only one in class who raised my hand because I knew the answer.

At the time, I filed that answer into my head so that I would never forget it. I've remembered that all my life. I always keep that in the forefront of my mind when I'm dealing with other people. I guess I became somewhat of a people-pleaser with the intention of being kind. I find it very difficult to say "No" when someone needs help.

I remember one of my managers had coached me to say "No" because I was having to work overtime in order to meet deadlines, and I was constantly helping others with their work or training them on how to use software so that they could complete their work. Clearly being a people-pleaser was disrupting my life.

However, some good did come of it in that I believe that being a people-pleaser helped me to learn about the true gifts that I bring to the world. First, because being a people-pleaser can bring on many things that you don't want in your life, I've now learned how to deal with those things. Second, by analyzing why I was a people-pleaser, I've been able to figure out what my purpose is for this world.

It took some soul searching to figure out that my passion is helping people to heal their lives, and I have a huge heart filled with love and kindness to help them do just that. When I saw the look of hopelessness in the eyes of the people that were in rehab with me, I realized that I see that look on many people in everyday life. I now know that I can help people to find their passion and start living instead of just existing. Oddly enough, it took having a stroke before I figured it out. Sometimes God just has to give you a solid whack in the head for you to wake up.

Living consciously had to become a priority in my life. I was letting life happen to me instead of being the director of the symphony of my life. I don't know when I stopped living consciously; I do know that it was a gradual process, and I didn't even notice it happening.

It's funny how life sneaks up on you and starts taking control without you even knowing it. Well, I wasn't going to let that happen anymore. I was back in the driver's seat, and I wasn't letting anyone or anything get in my way. I started asking myself questions about all of the books that were on my shelves and applying what I had learned. Below are some of the nuggets of knowledge that I gleaned and started living in my life.

What is your approach to Life?

Do you create your life or does your life just happen? Many people are "life sleep-walkers." They exist and life just happens to them. On the other hand, when you create your life, you are making conscious decisions about how and what happens in your life. Most of the time by making small changes every day, you will start to see your life change and start to take the course or path that you really want to go. When things start to go awry and you are consciously living, you make course corrections to get back on target.

As you start to make progress in living the life you deserve, you will start feeling happier. You will start achieving your goals and aspiring to bigger and better goals. Even when bad things happen to you, you know that if you go with the flow, you will start making the proper decisions, and that everything will be all right. You know that small detours will happen, and that you can get back on track once you've resolved the situation that appeared out of nowhere and threw you off track. Often times, the small detours are life lessons that will help you later on if you learn the lesson that was intended for you.

Our life journeys can be fun and exhilarating if we live through them and continue to learn everyday throughout our journey; or they can be hard and depressing if we wallow in our pain and become victims of life instead of learning, celebrating and living life to its fullest.

Blessings and Gratitude

We all have blessings in our life to be grateful for. What many of us don't take into account is that many of the bad things that have happened or the mistakes that we have made as we make our way through life are additional blessings in disguise. They are life lessons that we otherwise might not have learned if the mistake or bad thing had not happened. If we treat these life lessons as blessings and are grateful for them, we will reap a much richer harvest than if we wallowed in the pain of the lesson.

I had a stroke and could have played the victim role; however, I saw it as a blessing in disguise, and it helped me realize that I needed to live life consciously.

Some people resent the fact that something bad happened to them, and they become negative and unhappy. We've all heard the quote "What goes around comes around." This is true about life: if you give out negative vibes, you will get more negative vibes in return. As well as, if you give out positive vibes, you will get more positive vibes in return. Also, if you are grateful for your life lessons, and you apply the learnings, you will be more blessed.

❝ Forgiving the hurts from your past will make you happier.

I expect to pass through life but once.

If there can be any kindness I can

show, or any good thing I can do for any fellow being,

let me do it now, and not defer or neglect it,

as I shall not pass this way again. **❞**

~ *William Penn*

In the past, I used to let "past hurts" bother me. I felt that people were holding onto grudges about things that happened which I felt were untrue. This made me feel as if I was not good enough. "Past hurts" create a lot of unhappiness. The person you are holding the grudge against most of the time is already over what happened and your unhappiness is not hurting them. Do not continue to live a life full of grudges. You will start to feel like a victim and no good can come from that.

By letting go, you are freeing yourself from the negative energy that is holding you in the past. When you forgive them for whatever happened, you release the negativity that you have been holding. You don't have to talk to the person to do this. You just have to do it sincerely, and the heaviness from your heart will lift which will leave room for happiness and love to move in.

What is a victim mentality?

When I observed some of the people in my rehab program and saw the hopelessness in their eyes, I wanted to ask them how they felt, but I also did not want to bring up bad feelings. When I did start to have conversations with them, I found that they didn't think they would ever get better. When their families picked them up at the rehab center, I could see how much they enjoyed the care and attention they were getting from their families. Is it possible that they were not getting better because they did not want to give up this care and attention if they got their life back? I couldn't help but think that for some of these people that might be the case.

Having a victim mentality means that you are putting other people in charge of your happiness. When you put others in charge of your happiness, you also release yourself from feeling bad because things are not working out for you. A person with a victim mentality blames others for why they are not happy…..it is always someone else's fault. If you hold yourself accountable for your happiness, you choose to be happy and make the right things happen in order to maintain your level of happiness. Take responsibility for your own happiness!

How Can You Bring Hope and Happiness Back into Your Life?

First of all, you will need to take a look at what's going on in your life and figure out what's working that you can keep doing. Then decide what you need to change. The easiest way to identify what needs to change is to find where the pain is in your life. What are you avoiding? Who or what uses up your energy?

It's important to focus on things that are within our circle of influence. If you do not have control over what you need to change, you cannot change it. The hardest part of making these changes is realizing that only "you" can change. You cannot change someone else to make YOUR life work better. Identify how YOU can change to make the situation better.

Often times, it is a matter of changing how you perceive things which is very different from the perception of others. We can all see the exact same thing and see it differently. Police Officers will take statements from people who have observed an accident, and every statement will be different because each person sees what happened from their own personal perspective.

Only you have the power to choose what will make you happy in your life. When you make conscious choices, you stop doing the things that don't make you happy and start doing the things that do. I know that's easier said than done. Make small changes and the big changes will start to evolve; you will be amazed how quickly things will start to change for you.

What do I do when I've made course corrections, and I still don't get on target?

Great question….you are not alone, this happens to a lot of people. Actually, I would venture to say that it happens to most people. Sadly to say, a high percentage of people start to let life happen to them without even noticing that it is happening instead of creating the life they deserve. Many of us can live most of our adult lives doing this. Think about many of the people that you know at work, church or social acquaintances; do you think any of them are life-sleepwalkers?

Generally speaking, it is not a good idea to compare yourself to other people; I'm suggesting you do this only for the purpose of visualizing how

Restoring Your Beautiful Life

many people are life-sleepwalkers. Instead compare yourself against your goals and determine how close you are to achieving them. If you are not where you want to be, change what you are doing so that you start moving in the direction of your goals.

In some respects, I'm grateful that a stroke woke me up and prevented me from continuing to fall into the life-sleepwalkers trap.

Then there are the brave souls that will try to figure out what is stopping them. Most of the time they have limiting beliefs that are holding them back. They need to identify the limiting beliefs or barriers and learn to overcome them. Whole books have been written on how to identify and eliminate limiting beliefs. Let me share a few ways to identify your limiting beliefs with you:

~ Negative messages from family, friends, people with authority
~ Lack of self-love; for example, I'm too fat, I'm too old
~ Feeling not good enough
~ I do not deserve it
~ That's the way I am
~ Any statement with the word "should" in it
~ Lack of self-confidence
~ Think about some of the clichés that have became a part of you or
   stereotypes that you may be living up to

How do I overcome limiting beliefs?

Overcoming limiting beliefs can sometimes be as simple as changing your thought patterns. However, as many of us have learned, it's not always easy to change a thought pattern that you've held for a lifetime. Once again, you have to take it a step at a time.

First, identify the limiting beliefs and change your self-talk. For example, some people will say things like "I'm too old" or "I'm too fat" or "I don't deserve it". Review the list above and identify your limiting beliefs.

Then decide if it is a true statement or not; if it is a true statement, how can you make it into a positive statement? For example:

"I'm too old" can become "I've learned a lot over my lifetime, I can do anything I put my mind to." And then DO IT!

"I'm too fat" can become "I am working towards fitting into my perfect size of jeans." And then DO IT!

"I don't deserve it" can become "I deserve all good in my life."

Next, identify where the belief originated. You learned this belief somewhere; you were not born with it. For example, if it originated when you were growing up, you will not only need to change your self-talk but you will also need to be aware when you are around people that you grew up with that they may still make statements that support that limiting belief. You will need to remind yourself that what they are saying is NO LONGER TRUE for you.. You have to build in a plan to overcome anything, or anyone that might unknowingly sabotage your plan to remove your limiting beliefs.

Finally, changing self-talk or thought patterns takes consistent work. Keep re-enforcing your new belief by using positive affirmations and visualizations. Soon your life will blossom into the life of your dreams. Keep working towards what you want and eliminate what you don't want.

Do Positive Affirmations really work?

A positive affirmation is a way of putting into words what you want your current situation to be. In other words, it is a statement that describes in a positive way, in present tense what is possible. It must be stated in present tense because if you state it in the future, it will remain in the future, and you diminish your ability to attain it. An example of a positive affirmation: "I am happy living in a peaceful, safe environment." Once you've written your positive affirmation; you can inject more power into the affirmation by visualizing it in your mind.

Affirmations and visualizations certainly worked for me in overcoming the debilitating effects of a stroke. I'm convinced that incorporating them into my rehabilitation plan helped me to recover in less than half the time the doctors had predicted.

It has been proven that visualizing performing tasks is as good as actually doing the task. In the book Psycho-cybernetics, Maxwell Maltz describes that by visualizing yourself performing a task is the same as practicing performing the task over and over again. Athletes use visualization to practice when they have been hurt and cannot physically practice. Victor Frankl in his book, *A Man's Search for Meaning*, states that while he was a prisoner of war, he visualized himself playing golf every day. When he was released three years later, he played golf as if he had been playing every day. His handicap was lower than it had ever been. Clearly positive affirmations and visualizations work if used properly.

Why do I worry about what other people think?

66 Only when we are no longer afraid,

do we begin to live. 99

~ Dorothy Thompson

Most of the time when we are concerned about what other people think, we are either afraid of success or afraid of failure. In all actuality, people don't think about you as often as we think they do. They are probably worrying about what you are thinking, too.

What are you afraid of?

Dr. Wayne Dyer in one of his books states that FEAR is False Evidence Appearing Real. How true is that?   How many things are we afraid of that never happen?   Do not allow other people to take your power away.

66 Keep away from people who try to

belittle your ambitions.

Small people always do that, but the really

great people make you feel

that you too, can become great. 99

~ Mark Twain

Start moving towards your goals regardless of what anyone else will think. Seriously, does it matter what they think? And if it does, are you looking for recognition? If it is recognition that you are looking for, achieving a goal will get you more recognition then worrying about what other people think.

What's the worst that can happen if you succeed? Think about it and write it down. When you write it down it provides clarity and then you can decide if it is true for you. If the worst that can happen 'if you succeed' rings true for you, you can plan for it and be prepared to deal with it. If it is not true, stop worrying about it. Being worried and/or afraid will only hold you back from achieving your goal.

What's the worst that can happen if you fail? Once again, think about it, document it, and decide if the worst that can happen 'if you fail' really can happen? If it is true, be prepared to overcome it. If it is not true, stop worrying about it and move on. You will be happy you did, and you will be moving in the direction of your dreams.

Finally, have you heard of the flight or fight response? Psychologists have proven that people have an innate response that prepares the body to "fight" or "flee" from perceived attack, harm or threat to our survival including worrying about what other people might think. When we plan for something that might happen and are prepared, we lessen the impact on our life and the desire to "fight" or "flee." We can then flow through the situation instead of fighting with it.

It's so much easier to flow through situations than to fight our way through life. The last thing we want to do is to flee, that's when you find yourself "sleep-walking" through life instead of living consciously. When we flee, we let life happen to us instead of taking control of our life.

Whack in the Head to Wake me up

I've known everything I've written about in the preceding pages for many years; however, I wasn't living it. I had become a "life-sleepwalker," and I seriously needed a whack in the head to wake me up. It certainly was a painful big jolt and a huge lesson learned. I am now living my life consciously.

I still have a lot of work to do but I make progress every day. I also have a lot of good to do and many gifts to share with the world. I have learned to create boundaries on my time so that I can use my time more effectively. Instead of allowing life to take me wherever it wants to lead me, I am now making course corrections so that I stay on target with my dreams. I know that I am on the right path because I have learned to listen to my inner voice and guide.

Having a second chance to live the life of your dreams is a wonderful gift that cannot be taken lightly. I'm hoping this story will help someone not need to have a wake-up call like mine to get them back on the right path to live their life consciously. It's an honor to be able to live courageously and give to the world.

We've all been given unique gifts to share with the world. What's your unique gift? Do not waste your life!

TAMMY GYNELL LAGOSKI

Chapter 3:
Kaleidoscope

CHAPTER 3
Kaleidoscope

As children, many folks have had the joy of peering inside a kaleidoscope, slowly turning the scope until the black and gray shadows and fragments became an array of vivid colors and patterns. Life is like a kaleidoscope, ever changing from the bleak world of blacks and grays, which represent the dark pathways and the shadows of spiritual and physical sickness, depression, and loneliness, into the vibrant hues and designs which represent healing, peace, joy, and the beauty of being alive.

But, what happens when the scope sticks and no longer turns, and the pattern and shades became stuck in a bleak world, a world of spiritual, physical and emotional pain? How does an individual find the strength to turn the scope, releasing the bleakness and discovering the healing colors and patterns of life?

The answers are never easy, nor are they the same for one person or the next; therefore, the goal of this chapter is to share with you my experiences when the scope locked and life became nothing but shadows and darkness and the healing process that gave me strength to turn the kaleidoscope of life into a brilliant array of peace and healing as well as the appreciation for the many forms of friendship.

The book, *From Broken to Beautiful*, by Lisa A Hardwick brought back memories of my own childhood and the aloneness that seemed to plague a small, chunky and awkward young girl. Lisa and I had much more in common than one would realize. The obvious bit of connection or thread we shared was that of being neighbors.

In the winter when the fields were bare, one could look out the back door or kitchen window and see the farm house where Lisa grew up. Although Lisa is several years younger than me, we never played together or grew up as friends.

What we do have in common then is similar childhood experiences, not the same, but similar. Both Lisa and I were plagued with low self-esteem, childhood secrets and a broken family.

We attended the same grade school and shared the same teachers. Good teachers who meant well, but back then, did not have the knowledge, or training to work with children from abused or broken families.

In our area, the families farmed together, went to church, had potlucks, played cards, and attended school functions with their kids. In general, the families were hard working and caring folk, but it was rare to talk about personal issues such as an unfaithful spouse, domestic violence, or alcoholism.

The unspoken expectations were that one never revealed what went on behind closed doors. What would have happened when darkness settled in, and an individual peered into the windows of the house, what would they really see? Would it be perfection, or fractured lives and secrets so well hidden, no one ever knew they existed?

The scene is set, the darkness shrouding hidden secrets, what then becomes of the child living among the cloaked shelter of loneliness and abuse? What happens to the child who witnesses a drunken father beating her parent, throwing siblings into walls and was told, "You aren't good enough, don't you know how to do anything"? Perhaps the little waif was told "Why can't you be more like your cousin who makes straight "A's", can sing, dance, sew, etc.?"

Follow along with me and I will give you a glimpse into my home, a home with mixed signals of fun family times, and the dark side of alcoholism and abuse.

My mom married my stepfather the summer before my second grade then moved us to the family farm. The farm was a huge playground peppered with a big white barn, Black Angus cattle, an old corn crib that housed the farm tractors and wagons full of beans, as well as two old sheds, a large wooden garage painted white to match all the other out buildings, and lastly, miles of country roads to ride and explore. Mom had her hands full keeping my two brothers and I corralled.

Not long after we moved to the farm two sisters and a younger brother were added to the brood. As the oldest child of the family, it was my job to help watch over the younger tykes. My stepdad added to my mom's burden with his drunken rages and mood swings. As soon as my dad would step through the back door, we were able to gauge his frame of mind, which would then set the mood for the rest of the night.

One night when I was in the third grade, my dad came into my bedroom angry at something I said or did, clenched his hand into a fist and popped me square in the nose. Blood spurted out and down my face. My mother was furious and threatened to call the police if he ever hit me again. From that night on, he never hit me, but the mental abuse began.

Although from that night on I was spared from the physical abuse, my poor brothers were not. In addition to the mental abuse, they were knocked upside the head, punched in the face, and thrown into walls. Many nights my dad would toss mom into the refrigerator, clobber her in the head with the phone, and ram her into walls, shouting filthy names at her while hitting her.

Numerous nights, trembling in fear, my little body would slip in between my mom and dad trying desperately to protect her any way I could. In retaliation, my dad would push my mom and me out the back door and down the steps out into the bitter cold or smoldering heat and lock the door behind us as we stood sobbing in fear. With heads hung low we would head for the car in the garage where we hunkered down sometimes until the wee hours of the morning. Eventually, we would slowly head for the house hoping and praying the door would be unlocked. Sadly, there were times we were forced to stay out in the garage all night, in the rain, snow, bitter cold, or smoldering heat.

66 What we all are right now are victims of victims. **99**

~ Lisa A Hardwick

Thankfully, not all days and nights were fraught with alcoholic rages; in fact, sometimes my dad would gather all of us kids together, and we would pile in the turquoise Ford station wagon and head to town. How I loved those jaunts!

One of the stores we would clamor into would be Ben Franklin's. Man, that store had the largest color books a child could imagine and big boxes of crayons, too! One of my favorite treats happened to be the humongous (well, this kid thought it was) old fashioned Santa coloring book. To this day, I love those coloring books.

The next store we would head off to was Warehouse Sales. The store was full of clothes, toys, cleaning stuff, and grocery items. My dad would buy us jeans and tops along with tons of Snicker Bars, Milky Way, Three Musketeers and M&M's. What a treat!

One of the appliances missing from our household was a washer and dryer. Can you imagine how much laundry my mom had to wash for a household of six kids? Every week or so, the old station wagon was loaded up with laundry and kids, and off we went to the laundry mat in town. Luckily for us, the local Dairy Queen was next to the laundry mat. I can still taste those cones. To this day nothing can compare to the old DQ treats!

The customers in the laundry mat would sit and watch our antics and shake their heads in laughter or anger while we ran around the washer and dryers with the carts in tow. When the *I Love Lucy Show* would come on television, all six of us would sit down to watch the show. We would laugh and giggle at Lucy's comic displays. Over the years, those fun days became fewer as we finally got our very own brand new washer and dryer.

On several occasions my dad would holler, "Outside!" We would run like mad to the gravel driveway to play a game of basketball, or gather in the yard to play softball. My favorite position while playing softball was first base.

For some reason my skills when I was at home were outta this world. Unfortunately, when playing at school or the park, my skills seem to disappear and lacked the finesse one needed to play. In other words: I was a klutz. But that didn't keep me down, since playing "Annie, Annie Over" was my strong suit.

For those of you too young to recall; the game consisted of tossing a ball over a small shed and running around the other side and catching the ball. When the ball flew over the roof, we would scramble like mad to the other side and push aside anyone in our way then quickly grab the ball. Laughter and silly giggles would ensue from my classmates and me as we ran back to "home base." The good thing about this game ... I could practice at home and hone my skills until the next round at the play ground.

My siblings and I loved to perform. Many days you would find us outside using the back steps as our stage, singing, dancing and acting plain silly for each other, our parents, and my grandmother. In the fall after the beans had been harvested, we would head out to the corn crib, climb the old farm wagon and jump into the pile of soy beans. My poor uncle would get so frustrated with us, but we never seemed to get enough of "bean jumping."

If we weren't out in the corn crib, you could find us in the barn among the haystacks making forts and playing hide and seek. On days we were unable to play outside we would make forts using the furniture and blankets as our building materials. One of my favorite pastimes was playing jumping jacks. I could play that for hours.

Our farm house was a small bungalow with two original bedrooms; the third bedroom consisted of the porch being remodeled for my brothers' bedroom. At night, we would snuggle down in our respective rooms, the boys jumping up and down on their beds, my sister and I reading, or giggling at the stories we would make up for fun. Most households are quiet at night, but not ours. One brother would talk in his sleep, the other one would walk in his sleep and mom would have nightmares and holler out in her sleep.

One night, my mom started screaming. Of course being the protector, I ran out into the living room to see what had happened. Stuttering and shaking my poor mother called my dad at the Railroad Yard Office where he was a switchman. Suddenly, mom screamed into the phone, "There was a face looking in the kitchen window!" My dad jumped into his ole blue Chevrolet truck and headed home ready to fight whatever or whoever was lurking around the yard.

After arriving home, my dad walked around the house and yard, then opened the back door and came into the house laughing his head off ... a cow had gotten out of the pasture and decided to take a field trip. The "face" that had terrified my mother so much was a COW!

Another month or so went by, then mom heard someone at the back door in the wee hours of the morning. Once again, I hopped out of bed ready to go to battle and protect my mom. But thank goodness, nothing really transpired that night.

The last story in our adventurous nighttimes happened when I was in the fifth or sixth grade. My bed stretched out in front the window in order to take advantage of the summer breezes. Thankfully, that night, my windows were closed and securely locked, providing a barrier of protection from whatever night creatures were lurking around in the shadow of the trees. Crawling into bed, I plumped my pillow, pulled and tugged at the covers tucking them all around me. Hunkering down under the blankets I drifted off to sleep, but not for long.

A noise permeated my being and suddenly I awoke to a strange sound. The noise sounded like a crow bar creaking and wrenching at my window. I crept out of my bed on all fours and crawled to my bedroom door, stood up and ran for all my might to my parents' bedroom.

Stuttering in fear, my father finally got the story out of me, only to proclaim, "It was just a tree limb brushing the window." My response was, "But Dad, do trees run?" My mighty and fearless dad grabbed his shot gun, went outside and explored the parameters of the house. He never did find anyone, but this little girl knew "trees don't run."

> **"** There is so much love in your heart
>
> that you could heal the entire planet.
>
> But for now, let us use this love to heal YOU. **"**
>
> ~ *Louise Hay*

By the time my sophomore year came around, the arguments, beatings and drinking seemed to escalate. One night my mom had had enough, packed us all up and moved us outside of town into a drafty two bedroom trailer. When the wind howled, the tattered curtains would gently blow in the breeze. The trailer didn't have much furniture: a couch, kitchen table and two beds. Not much for a crew of six kids and a parent.

During my sophomore year I took Spanish I. This class was very difficult for me, but I loved the class. Perhaps, that is why my Spanish teacher took pity on a young girl. Bless her heart, Ms. W. arranged to have a tutor come to my home in order to raise my grade. The young lady that tutored me was an upperclassman, a Majorette (baton twirler) from a good family and beautiful.

Embarrassment plagued me when my tutor came to the dilapidated trailer. Sitting at the kitchen table, I would look around the room and see the curtains moving in the cold breeze, holes in the furniture and a bare forlorn kitchen. But my tutor was very kind and patient with me, never showing disgust or horror at the shape of our home. Once the Spanish lessons began, my attention was captured and swept up in pronouns, pronunciation of words, and the graphic descriptions she painted of Mexico and Spain.

Although the tutoring was excellent and comprehensive, my final grade was a "C." That didn't deter Ms. W. one bit; in fact, she wanted me to sign up for Spanish II. Of course, the teacher probably said this to all her students; regardless, it made a young lady feel wanted and valued. But for some reason, instead of taking Spanish II, I signed up for an English class. What a big mistake! My English teacher turned out to be a French teacher who hadn't taught English in years. Most days, she either spoke in French, or wrote on the chalkboard in French. This class had the opposite affect on a young insecure young lady. For instance, it was hard to speak up in class. Most days, I sat quietly and listened to the teacher, worked hard to keep up, but no matter what I attempted to do, it wasn't good enough.

Since Junior High, my grades in English had been "B's," but by the end of the first semester my grades were failing. One of the reasons given for my failure was the lack of class participation. How humiliating for an impressionable teenager: to be flunked and expected to retake a class in her senior year.

My saving grace during this time was my nurse's aide training class. This class opened up an opportunity to work in a local nursing home; which in turn, took me away from the arguments, tension and worries at home. My job at the nursing home evolved around caring for the patients on the skilled care wing where the patients were either bedridden or wheelchair bound.

The majority of the people had dementia, cancer or multiple sclerosis, like my friend, Dorothy, who was a classy and gentle lady. Chatting with her on a daily basis was rewarding and fulfilling. Hopefully, my visits brought a bright spot to her days as well.

While working at the nursing home, I had the honor of working off and on in PT (Physical Therapy) which was an honor. Why? Only the "good" aides were allowed to work in that department! What a boost to my low self-esteem to be trusted enough to work in a respected department.

❝ If you are confident of whom you really are

there's no need to prove it. **❞**

~ Healing Art

Memory is failing me, but it was either my junior or senior year in high school when I decided to try out for the Trojets (Pom Pom Squad). I can recall putting my text books in my locker and walking down the corridor to the gym. Once arriving at the doors, I peeked in looked around at the "popular girls," turned around, ran to the school office, called home to ask my mom to come pick me up at the front doors.

Later on I mentioned to the sponsor, Mrs. H., that I made it to the gym, but "got cold feet and left." Mrs. H. looked at me and told me I should have tried out, I probably would have made the squad. Can you believe it, me on the squad! This teenager felt honored and proud of the compliments Mrs. H. had given me. Yes, she probably said that to all the girls, but at that moment in time, this girl felt special. What would have happened if my destructive thoughts were non-existent?

The nursing home was my saving grace, but my church was my salvation. It was at church that I made friends, went to church day camp, youth group, and sang in the youth choir which enabled us to travel to churches and nursing homes for concerts. The adults at the church were always planning something for the kids. How dedicated they were to teaching us and nurturing our spirit. My church family was my refuge.

Perhaps, my Sunday school teacher, Mrs. M., thought otherwise. What do I mean by that statement? Well, my "group of kids" wasn't the easiest of kids to be around. We were loud, giggly and very ornery. One Sunday morning a few of the girls climbed out on the roof, while the rest of the class locked the Sunday school teacher in the closet. To this day we still laugh about this incident. Poor old Mrs. M.

It was my church, the First Baptist Church, where I learned about Jesus and his love towards all individuals. It was also at the church that I witnessed the faith of my mother grow and blossom. My mom was my inspiration, my role model; although she was facing adversity at home, mom's faith grew and was unshakeable regardless of the darkness. God would shield her, protect her, and guide her through the darkness.

I would be remiss if I didn't give credit to Mom Stewart and the unconditional love she gave a young girl. Mom Stewart had an open door policy for me. No matter what, I always had a home to retreat to when life was a hardship.

Mrs. F., and her daughters, who I will refer to as Ann, Cher and Marie, also opened their home and hearts to a young waif. Thanks to them, a sense of work ethic was instilled in me as Ann and I would deliver newspapers in the dark hours of morning. Cold, bitter days, it didn't matter. The paper had to be delivered, and Ann bless her heart, did her job well.

After papers were delivered and morning chores completed, we would traipse off to school. The jaunt seemed to take forever on foot, perhaps it was about 10-15 minutes tops, but whatever it was, it was long.

Ann's sister, Cher, was the sweetest girl and one of the prettiest girls in school. She also had the patience of a saint for a young girl with puppy dog eyes who would follow her around the house, hang out in her bedroom watching as she put her make-up on and curled her long blonde hair.

Ann's Aunt Louise (not her real name) and Cousin Rose invited me to their home numerous times where we played games, ate popcorn, drank soda and watched television. Louise's house was always filled with love and acceptance.

ﾉℐ Restoring Your Beautiful Life

66 Painful experiences are not meant to linger.

They are meant to teach us what they need to teach us,

and then dissolve into the realm of soft-focus memory. **99**

~ Marianne Williamson

Senior year came around, and it was time to think about college. One day, I approached my school counselor to talk about my dreams and goals. Since I loved working at the nursing home, my dream was to continue to work in the healthcare field. Thus, my heart was set on attending school to become an LPN (Licensed Practical Nurse). The training was only nine months, didn't look like it would cost too much, and the best part, I could continue working at the nursing home.

Well, that was my dream not the counselor's goal. To this day, my heart cringes when I hear the words he had to share with me, out of his great wisdom and knowledge of my academics, "You cannot go to nursing school, you would flunk." Yes, that was the word he used: Flunk. My heart was broken.

Several years later as a middle-aged adult, I did pursue college. During my tenure in college, my grades were "good enough" to get me on the Dean's List and into Psy Chi and Phi Gamma Mu Honor Societies. Sadly, due to health reasons, I had to withdraw my last year.

The point is this: Part of me wanted to call up that old counselor and say, "What do you think of me now?" Petty as that may sound, the vulnerable teenager and adult would have loved to be validated in his eyes. Validation. How many folks search for validation or confirmation that they matter to someone, that they are pretty, smart, worthy of belonging and being loved? What happens if that individual does not find the acceptance and love they need? Some people may turn to alcohol, drugs, sex, or violence. Thankfully, my faith guided me away from that lifestyle, shielded and protected me when life seemed bleak and colorless.

This does not mean my life has been void of disappointments, anger, hurt or low self-esteem. Contrarily, my life has been a journey of the bad and good, including unemployment, divorce, several moves, illness, severe depression and an attempt of suicide.

Fear is a great enemy of the human brain and soul, as is failure. In other words, fear of being rejected because of my looks, lack of smarts or education, not being sophisticated enough to blend in with a new community, and fear of not succeeding in college.

My strength, my faith in God took a nosedive, and I felt alone in my new community. I found it hard to make friends since school took up the majority of my time, and the rest of the time I was sick. Being sick all the time and not having a social network plunged me into a deep depression and my suicide attempt.

For a long time, I blamed the community we moved to for my loneliness and rejection. My brain kept telling me, this community is closed, you have to be born here in order to belong, to be an integral part of the community. Perhaps that is the truth, but what would have happened if I had been proactive instead of reactive? Would my life have been different?

It is easy to sit here and reflect on what might have happened, what could have been, but in truth, it is what did happen that matters. I lost sight of my faith and wallowed in darkness and self-pity, which resulted in my "field trip" to the Psychiatric Ward (or Psy ward) where my eyes were opened, and my heart found solace and healing.

The Psy ward was a unique place to be and provided an opportunity to observe the other patients, especially for a Psychology major. The wing, which was on lock down, had drug addicts, young teens and adults using Heroin and Meth, a man who tried to kill someone along with himself, in addition to the alcoholic and severely depressed patient.

We all had something in common: the need to belong, to be accepted, and self-destructive behaviors. In essence, we were all broken and waiting for someone to put us back together again, to restore and rejuvenate our minds, hearts and souls. Sadly, not all the patients were on a road of recovery and restoration. The Psy ward was a pit stop forced upon them, a place to pretend, a place to get out of as soon as possible.

How sad, that the hearts and souls were so damaged that healing could not take place. Healing restored and a life re-purposed means work is required. Work that I was forced to do while being locked in the Psy ward.

What a metaphor: "locked in." That is what I was, locked in the prison of my own mind and feelings – feelings of rejection, sorrow and selfishness. The goal of treatment was to search the dark recesses of my mind and to destroy the negative thoughts that seemed to permeate my being, keeping me from growing and becoming the person God meant me to be.

At first, my body was too weak, and my mind too tired to focus on healing. But one day while in the gathering room, a book resting on the piano caught my eye. The book was about prayer and healing. Was this an accident? Of course not, it was meant to be. While reading the book my heart and soul became alive.

I had so many thoughts to write down, but the only thing to write with was a crayon and the sheet of paper the nurse was kind enough to give me. During one of my calls home, I asked my husband to bring me something to write with and a composition notebook, ones without metal spirals. Bless his heart, he brought me a notebook, but it had spirals.

The nurse let me have the notebook on one condition: the sheets of paper had to be torn out before my husband left for the night. So my fingers quickly ripped out the pages while trying not to tear the pages apart. By the time the visit was over, I had a nice stack of papers to take with me to my room.

Several times a day, I would write and study the scriptures. God didn't leave me, I left him. His love was unconditional, it didn't depend on how smart I was, how pretty or skinny I was, but on ME, the person he created.

After a few days in the Psy ward, the Psychiatrist would meet with the patients. He was a quiet man with a sense of humor and patience. One of the first questions, I asked the poor man was: "What type of method do you use when working with your patients?" The Psy student was trying to show him she was savvy. How funny was that, my friends!

Gently he probed, questioned and at times sat in silence as my mouth chattered on and on about loneliness, rejection and insights that were garnered from my studies and reflections during my quiet times. The Psychiatrist bless his heart, allowed me to go home early. To this day, I am thankful for his quiet demeanor and analysis regarding my treatment and healing process.

> **66** Forgiveness is a gift to myself.
> I forgive, and set myself free. **99**
> *~ Louise L. Hay*

It has taken a lot of courage to open up and share the vignettes of my life due to embarrassment and pride. One is supposed to be strong and never show the effects of failure and depression with strangers or family members. Why? Because it is better to keep "certain" situations private and deal with them the best way that one can. Embarrassment is akin to pride when one worries about what others may think of your weaknesses; hence, the fear of opening up reaching out and speaking from the heart.

When Lisa and I were growing up across the fields from each other, what would have happened if she and I were capable of developing a friendship built on trust? Would we have taken the opportunity to expose our hidden secrets? Perhaps yes, perhaps not. Yes, it would have been nice to have someone to share my stories with, but that wasn't the plan at the time.

In fact, Lisa and I had different life lessons to learn, thus our paths were guided in opposite directions. As adults we have grown to represent dissimilar situations so that we may teach, guide and nurture different populations. Our lives are like a piece of artwork. For instance, what one perceives as artwork, the next person in line sees as rubbish. Likewise with my life experiences and Lisa's.

This does not mean our situations are any less significant than the other's; on the contrary, the stories of our life are masterpieces that God created from the rich color of our lives and the dark contrast of the heartache that we endured.

66 My Greatest fear had come to be, I was broken. **99**

~ Lisa A Hardwick

My childhood was bittersweet, and after all these years, the memories have dulled the sting of my father's words, as age has softened my father's heart. A few years ago my father apologized to my mother for his behavior and abuse throughout the years they were married. Although divorced, my dad has never missed a family function.

Although I love my dad, there are days when I wish what he felt for me was the same as he felt for my younger siblings. My sisters and brother share the same blood as my dad, thus they are his kids, and I am the child he adopted. Knowing this does hurt at times, yet I am thankful for my dad and all my siblings.

Sadly, my dad has early stages of Alzheimer's and his memory is good one minute, yet the next minute he cannot recall where he is. For example, sometimes he thinks he is in Indiana, but in reality he is at home. Should one remain angry and bitter at the person that created the heartache in one's life, or should one open their heart enough to forgive?

God wants us to forgive, especially when one is old, confused and vulnerable. If one chooses not to forgive, then the heart remains cracked and perhaps broken. Thus, complete healing is not allowed to take place. How does one find the ability to forgive? The answer is not always the same for all people, but a good start is praying and having faith that God will work through your road blocks to forgiveness and hopefully open the door to healing. Is this easy? No, it has taken many years to find forgiveness in my heart for my dad.

As for the other folks and events in my life, it is a daily battle not to give in to resentment, blame and anger. During times of frustration, it is imperative to stop, pray and listen to God. Listen for his gentle and soothing words and allow them to soften your heart. The next step is to put Self aside and focus on how you can help someone else. The action may be small, such as doing dishes, making a phone call, buying groceries or running errands for someone. Regardless of the action one chooses, the outcome is the same; instead of focusing on Self, the focus is another individual and their needs and concerns.

The following quote is from Path of the Soul Destiny Card Reading:

Do you know how beautiful you truly are?

It is time to stop hiding from the world. The Universe is calling you. You have so much to offer, so much to give. This card is a reminder for you to see who and what you truly are. You are a part of the One. You are beautiful and perfect in every way. When you hide yourself you are withholding, not only your energy - but your Love. Love for yourself and Love for others. Embrace yourself and all your quirks - we all have them! Let yourself be free. Let yourself shine.

Let yourself shine, allow yourself to be free of the past, the anger and the low self-esteem. It is time to control the Kaleidoscope of life. Will the scope remain stuck in the dark abyss of life's ugliness, or will the scope turn and reveal the beauty of life, and the peace that God has in store for you? Personally, I chose to turn the scope and accept the beauty of self, and the Holy Spirit.

Molly Weleski

Chapter 4:
Circle Of Forgiveness

CHAPTER 4
Circle of Forgiveness

Grinning from ear to ear I awake from the depths of a good night's sleep. If people were to see me at this time they would be quite intrigued about what I was dreaming of. These days I have the luxury – yes, luxury! – of awakening at 5a.m. I remember a time when I could barely drag my butt out of bed at 7:45 a.m. Strange how a change in perspective changes your whole entire life!

My big-ass grin is from knowing all is well in my world. I have love, yes I have IT! I now know the secret of where to find it! It is inside of me; where it has been all the time, talk about being oblivious! How can someone go through an entire forty-eight years of existence and not know where love is? That is totally absurd to me now.

> **66** If we really love ourselves,
>
> everything in our life works. **99**
>
> ~ Louise L. Hay

When I awake, I take the time for gratitude.

I thank God for my family and how precious they are to me, how many lessons I've learned from them, and all the lessons I will continue to learn. Through so much love and so much pain we have come to where we are now. My life is a testament to the thought that some of God's greatest gifts are *unanswered prayers*. This moves me to think of Garth Brooks and his song Unanswered Prayers, which runs through my mind at least once a week. Thanks, Garth, for hosting the meeting of our minds.

Of course I THANK GOD for all others in my life that I love, who love me, those people that encourage me by just being available if I need them, who cheer me on whether it is college cheerleader style, a mother-like fashion or just a smile and a quiet, good-for-you. I am just as grateful for those same people who are there for me to reciprocate those same soul supporting actions.

> **66** Encouragement is the oxygen of the soul. **99**
>
> ~ George M. Adams.

The next on my list of gratitude in the morning, flannel sheets. YES they come third on my list. Is it right for a self proclaimed spiritual person to care so much about something that is materialistic? I guess I have a ways to go on my spiritual path! Maybe it's just because I am laying on them and enjoying their comfort that they come to mind. But my family would probably argue with that because they are well aware of my love for flannel. If there is anything in my world that is materialistically irreplaceable, it is flannel. My bedding makes me feel safe and loved! I think about the people that were involved in making these pampering remnants that soothe and snuggle my physical being every night keeping my body warm and oh so comfortable. Do they know how often I think of them and ask for God to bless them? Are they having a good life? Are they feeling my blessings? I can only affirm that they are.

Next, I am thankful for all the people in my life that have had a hand in teaching me those difficult lessons, some of which seemed to have taken me forever to learn. I have been more than a difficult student at times. Yes, I do *thank* these people. I used to see them as DIFFICULT, I swore at them silently, and openly raged about them to any captured audience, which was usually my family, friends and sometimes coworkers.

If I only had powers to somehow hex them, those were the really mean ones. Oh to have the powers of Samantha Stephens on Bewitched! When desperate, I would just sit quietly in a pity puddle and wish them away. I would continue my theatrics swirling in a sea of resentment. I now know the only common denominator in those equations was me! I was having so much DIFFICULTY learning those lessons. Those lessons were and are ways to find out what I don't know about myself and truly what I don't like about myself.

66 Everything that irritates us about others

can lead us to an understanding of ourselves. **99**

~ *Carl Jung*

I continue my mantra of thanks:

I am thankful that I am safe, comfortable, and all my needs are met. It is surprising after contemplating your life, how little you really do have to complain about it.

I am thankful for my work that lends itself to my creativity. It is a right of everyone to have work that they are passionate about and that they look forward getting to and going to.

> 66 The portal of healing and creativity
>
> always takes us into the realm of the spirit. 99
>
> ~ Angeles Arrien

I thank the spiritual community for holding a space. For all those people, mentors, spiritual gurus that were and are willing to put themselves out there with their spiritual beliefs, paving the way to the healing of the universe.

> 66 If you knew who walks beside you
>
> on this path that you have chosen,
>
> fear would be impossible. 99
>
> ~ A Course in Miracles

Then I thank God again for my family, my husband and kids. Not sure why, but I am always compelled to give thanks for them twice in the morning! I guess it is because I wasn't quite sure my family & I would survive.

I remember when I was sixteen, I decided then that I wanted to be a mother – not right then and there, but eventually. Some of my friends thought I was so crazy even spending my time thinking of being a Mom when there were shops to explore, boys to meet, and fun to be had. When the time was right, I was going to be the best mother ever…but how would a person measure that? I'm not sure. It's funny how a person perceives things as so simple at that age. But I just knew that I would be a better Mom than the Mom I had. At that time I was quite bitter and had a whole lot of judgment for my Mother. I perceived her to be cold and abusive. Only once did I hear her say she loved me, and that was when she was drunk. I have now come to realize that she was doing the best she could. How could she love me if she didn't love herself? How could she teach me how to love myself if she didn't know self-love?

My Mom was doing the best she could with the knowledge and understanding that she had. As Louise L. Hay says, "we are all victims of victims." I think of my Mom poetically at times, thinking that she suffered so I might have the soul lessons I needed to learn in this lifetime. I have since made peace with her after all these years. But at the time I was adamant that I was never going to be like her.

As a girl of sixteen, my mom found herself pregnant, so she married the father of her unborn child, a Rifleman from the Canadian Army. She went on to have eight children, I being the seventh. From what I have learned, she lived with depression even before I was born but was never professionally diagnosed. For many years she self-medicated with alcohol and died as a result when I was twenty-eight.

Our family life was less than perfect, as with all other families. I had grown up in a family full of shame. We were poor. Most people thought that my parents had too many children, given that they couldn't take care of them. We were not a "morally fit family." There was physical, sexual and emotional abuse. There was no trust in our household. There were always mind games going on. My home life was quite unpredictable most of the time.

There were pregnancies out of wedlock. My youngest brother was born with a congenital heart condition. Just as he was starting to get well and free of constant viruses, one of my sisters was in a car accident that left her in the hospital for months in critical condition. For some time, she felt the effects of it both physically and emotionally. At about that same time, a brother ended up in jail for petty theft. It was extremely shameful. We couldn't hide that secret, everyone seemed to know. There were also undiagnosed mental illnesses that were easier to hide and were self-medicated with alcohol or drugs.

As a child I remember being so ashamed and secretive about who we were and what we did or didn't do. The secrecy and shame was overwhelming and almost suffocating at times.

I was going to do better. I was going to be better. My children were going to feel secure and loved. My children were going to have the best Mom ever!

My husband, Kim, and I were married in April of 1986, and, of course, we wanted children as soon as possible. My heart would break every month when I found out I wasn't pregnant. I was so scared, what if I wasn't able to conceive? What would happen then? We didn't have money for fertility treatments. Each month I would become increasingly anxious. My heart

Restoring Your Beautiful Life

would race, my throat would constrict, and my breath would become tight and short just at the thought of never being able to have children. I was desperate to have a baby.

Within this time my sister, to whom I was really close at the time, was told she was going to have her FIFTH child! I can still remember the moment clearly. I was in the doctor's waiting room with her, I didn't even know she was suspecting she was pregnant, but perhaps she didn't want to say anything because she knew how desperately I wanted that same circumstance.

Don't get me wrong, I was happy for her, I just wished that I was expecting, too. It just seemed to be one of those questions a person asks. Why can some people get pregnant and others not? Why not me? I had a tremendous fear. Was this God telling me I wasn't good enough to become a Mother? I had such deep insecurities. Intense feelings of not being good enough. Shame of everything and anything, even if I couldn't attach these feelings to any particular thing that I had done or the way that I was. How unfortunate for the Doctor to have a patient like me. I wanted a baby, and I wanted it right then. I was almost to the point of harassing him. For some reason he seemed to take it in stride, never getting irritated with me. Maybe he did, and I just didn't notice because I was so obsessed. That could be a definite possibility.

I started tracking my ovulation; I read anything I could get on fertility and the reasons for infertility. I was consumed with getting pregnant. This anxiety I experienced would suck me into a vortex of deep despair. I now know that through the law of attraction, I was attracting my circumstances. I was so fearful of not being able to conceive, I was fostering a situation of NOT BEING ABLE TO CONCEIVE! How could I be the best Mom ever if I couldn't have a family?

I remember the day the doctor told me I was pregnant, it was so unbelievable. I really, really couldn't believe it. I made him show me the paper with the test results. Thank you God! Thank you for this blessing, for answering my prayers. I was in heaven! I had waited so long. My dreams of a family were coming true.

But my euphoria slowly turned and inevitably neurosis had crept in. I didn't trust this process. I didn't trust the universe. Hey! I hadn't even heard of these concepts then. My thoughts were fast and furious. What if something happens during this pregnancy? What if I have a miscarriage, what if my baby has special needs?

After nine months of worries, Kim and I were so blessed to welcome a little boy who we named Dustin. He was a fussy little guy, and shortly after he was born, he was diagnosed with colic that continued until he was six months old. He also had a few minor health issues which required minor surgeries that were performed early in his life and left him practically unscathed. It is surprising to me now that my pregnancy was full term, and that he didn't have any major health issues.

Having a colicky baby kept me up every night. Kim was working away from home and was only home on weekends. I was weary and sleep deprived and found it hard to sort out my feelings and thoughts. I didn't have anyone to call on for relief. Everyone I knew had little ones themselves at home. Most of my friends and family were at least an hour away. Some didn't even have transportation.

In hindsight, I don't know whether I would have accepted any help anyways. I know I would have seen it as sign of weakness. Remember, I was going to be the best Mom ever! Super Moms didn't need any help. Martyrdom was the way of my world!

Although I so adored being a Mother, I didn't welcome unsolicited advice. So many people had so much to say and so many suggestions. He needs to be held more often. You pick him up so much you are going to spoil him. Feed him, he's hungry. Don't feed him, you are making him sick. Take him to the doctor. Naw, he doesn't need a doctor.

It was like they didn't have any confidence in me. They were mirroring what I felt. All of a sudden I became more fearful than usual, to the point of panic. I kept thinking I am responsible for this little guy, but I have no confidence in my ability to care for him or rear him. It hit me like a Mack truck. I kept my fears hidden, even from Kim.

I moved forward as a mother, trying to do my best. It was like when you close your eyes and hope for the best when opening a can of pop that might explode. I just kept going forward taking one day at a time, sometimes just one hour at a time. I would busy myself so as not to have to think of what was going on around me.

I would often go out of the way to prove I was a good mother, always putting my needs last. I would host children's parties and make sure Dustin was exposed to all types of learning activities as well as social activities. It is quite ironic when I look back on that part of my life. Here I was, trying to socialize him when at the time I was withdrawn and unapproachable. I didn't want anybody to get to know me. They would find out all of my flaws and see past my façade.

As time went on, I adjusted to motherhood and felt quite comfortable with all my insecurities around being a Mother. They were quite similar to the rest of my insecurities. Our life became normal. Well, it was OUR normal. Of course we wanted a sibling for Dustin so within a year we were trying to conceive again and were on yet another quest. Although I became anxious about it, the mere fact that I had had a successful pregnancy gave me a boost of optimism for being able to conceive again. It took a few months before we found out I was pregnant. Euphoria hit again! We were delighted to share the great news! Life went on.

Oh my God! Suddenly and horrifically, I felt piercing in my lower abdominal area and down through my pelvis. No Molly, I told myself, this was just the muscles adjusting to your pregnancy. I have nothing to worry about. I had experienced something like this when I was pregnant with Dustin. But then again, this was more of a pulling sensation. I tried to convince myself that all was well. Not every pregnancy is the same. This one is different. It could be different. I had a flurry of thoughts and questions mixed with scenarios of denial.

The morning went along. I was anxious and trembling. I busied myself as usual, so as not to think of what could be the outcome. Then again more pain. I was having contraction-like cramping, intense clenching of my uterus. There was no denying the situation. Something was seriously wrong. I hadn't given much thought to the physical pain of a miscarriage. In a few short minutes I was sitting in the bathroom, and I was passing clots. No, this can't be happening! I had never heard anyone talk of what actually happens physically, not to mention emotionally. How very sad to see your hopes and dreams literally being flushed.

The whole process of the miscarriage was a dehumanizing experience, both for our unborn child and for me as well. You have by all accounts a baby, a real baby inside of you. It might not look like a full term baby, but to me it was still my baby. The whole event seems to be inhuman, and so, so, very cold.

I rushed to the hospital only to find out that my fears had come true. I had had a miscarriage. The medical staff were quite matter-of-fact. It was like I was having a routine procedure, not unlike getting a wart removed from the sole of your foot. They were witnessing the hours after the death of what signified my future, my hopes and, my dreams. Didn't they know I was dying inside? Didn't they care? I look back now and see that the Universe was supporting me in the belief that I held; that the world was cold and unsupportive.

The following days and weeks were a haze of anger, grief and questions. Did I pick something up that was too heavy? Did I reach too far up in the cupboard? Maybe it was my genes. Was it something I ate? Something I drank? No, I was so careful - I thought. Maybe Kim and I should have had genetic testing before trying to conceive, but I hadn't even heard of it then. It was my fault. I berated myself. I should have known all these things. The sense of failure was simply overwhelming. This guilt was eating me alive. I kept on thinking that it was a punishment for something, I must have done something wrong. I was exhausted. The cloud of profound grief never lifted.

Because of my background in Psychiatric Nursing, I knew my state of mind wasn't at all healthy. But then it would be so shameful to seek out mental health for myself. What would anybody think if they knew? How does it look for someone trained in mental health to be in the depths of depression? But, my love for Dustin gave me the courage to go ahead with it. I didn't want him to have to grow up with a Mother that couldn't function. I sought out a Psychiatrist and made an appointment.

Her office happened to be on the Psychiatric Unit of the City Hospital. I remember praying: "Please God, don't let me run into anybody I know." I don't know how I managed to get to her office because my eyes were kept to the floor when I saw someone coming towards me.

I finally made my way across to the very back of the unit where her office was. As I sat down, the sun that warmed my face gave me a glimmer of hope. I thought okay, I got myself here, that was the hard part.

She heard my story of my miscarriage and how it had affected me. She started telling me that a woman like me does not need any more children to fulfill her life. What I needed to do was concentrate on a career. One that would make me independent, a professional career of sorts.

During the session the phone rang, and she actually took the call! She was elated with the news from caller, congratulating her on her achievements. The call seemed to last forever, and any hopes I had that this was going to be a catalyst to my recovery was crushed. After getting off the phone she proceeded to relay the good news to me. Her daughter had just received news that she received a 4.0 on all her university courses!

I could hardly believe what was happening. Was this a joke? Was I on some kind of sick version of "Candid Camera"? With my hopes dashed, and the psychiatrist still celebrating her daughter's good news, the session ended. She gave me a prescription for anti-anxiety medication and sent me on my way. She fulfilled my thoughts that no one was there to support me, and no one understands me.

After a couple of days of being drugged and in a haze of medication, I threw the drugs away and decided I would get better on my own. I had to do it alone; there was no one in the world that could help me. I busied myself. I read some self help books. I watched any T.V. episode that talked about how to deal with anxiety, depression, and miscarriage. Clinging on to any information that resonated with me, I tried to stay as positive as possible. Dustin was my saving grace. Eventually I got back to my normal. It was time to try again. The doctor gave me the go ahead to try to conceive. I had mixed feelings. At times I didn't know whether I wanted to try or not. What if I had another miscarriage again? What if it led to another bout of depression? That wouldn't be good for Dustin. Was I being selfish, or was it selfish not to try?

Kim and I decided to take a chance and try again. Wow! Within just a couple months I was pregnant again. I was anxious but everything seemed to be going well. I was in my second trimester when I went for a routine examination. After the blood work came back my doctor's nurse phoned to say they had scheduled me for an ultrasound. She said there was really nothing to worry about, that my hCG levels were just a little high. I was due for an ultrasound in the near future anyway, so we may as well do it then. I wasn't really worried. I was thinking I was past the three-month worry stage, which is when most miscarriages happen.

After the ultrasound, I was told to immediately meet my doctor at the hospital. I knew this wasn't good. The doctor met us at the hospital and proceeded to inform us that my pregnancy was a "Molar Pregnancy." What? I had never heard of such a thing!

He quietly told us that our baby had died. It had no chance of surviving. It was a hydatidiform mole, which is a growing mass of tissue inside the uterus that will not develop into a baby. It is the result of abnormal conception. A hydatidiform mole may be either complete or partial. A complete is usually due to one sperm fertilizing an egg which has no genetic information, so there is not enough genetic material present. A partial is usually due to two sperm fertilizing one normal ovum (which should not usually happen). This means that there is too much genetic material present. There can also be too much trophoblastic tissue which overtakes the growth of any fetal tissue, and the fetus does not develop normally. In my case, it was a partial. I thought I was hearing a script from a horror film.

I was immediately admitted into the hospital and given drugs to "expel the products of conception." My baby was now called a "product of conception"! At the time I wondered about the medical phraseology surrounding miscarriages. Was it intended to give me peace of mind or them? Maybe it was a little of both, but I don't think it succeeds at any.

My husband waited with me until I sent him home. I thought Dustin would need him more than I would. I was being a very good Mother, putting his needs before mine, or so I thought. I was again affirming that the Universe didn't support me.

The night was long, and the ward was dead silent which was very unusual for such a busy hospital. I lay there praying that it would all be over soon. Maybe I was just dreaming. Could it be? Suddenly, there was just a bit of pain, a need to push, and then it was all over.

I lay there alone. I had given birth to my baby. No one was around. The Universe was there again to support me in my thoughts; that I had to go it alone. That I was strong enough to do it alone. That I didn't need anyone's help. I called the nurse, and she came in. I couldn't talk I was crying so much, I just pointed down between my legs. With a look of pity and concern, she nodded and said she would take the 'tissue." She seemed like such a nice person. I felt pity and compassion for her for having to put her in such an uncomfortable position.

When would this nightmare end? Would it ever end? She gave me a sedative which gave me some relief until the next morning when the Universe again totally supported my belief that I considered the nightmare never ending. The doctor came in and explained that with this type of pregnancy comes a risk of cancer called Choriocarcinoma. He went on that there is a risk that some of the tissue from the mole can slough off and can metastasize to other parts of your body including your lung, liver or brain. Therefore, I would need close follow-up to monitor for this.

Follow-up consisted of a chest x-ray, a physical examination every two weeks until the uterus returned to normal then every three months for a year, and, most importantly, weekly hCG blood levels for six weeks then monthly for a year. If all went well, I could look at getting pregnant after a year. I remember sobbing uncontrollably all the way home, which was a 40-minute drive. I could hardly gain enough control to walk into my house.

No one talked about my miscarriage. It was taboo. If no one talks about it, does that mean it didn't happen? If no one talks about what could become cancer, does that mean it won't happen? I was grieving for my baby that I would never

Restoring Your Beautiful Life

know. I was grieving for the loss of my future as the Mom of the baby who has died. I was grieving not just because of what I had lost but because of what would never be. People just shied away from any conversation about it, whether it was the loss, the sadness, the vulnerability of it.

It was a very low time in my life, not just because of what happened, or what could happen, but for what people said or didn't say. Someone who I deeply loved thought I was lying about it being a pregnancy. She told family and friends that it wasn't a pregnancy at all, that it was JUST a tumor, and I was being overly dramatic. I was never a trusting person, but this affirmed my thoughts, that NO ONE can be trusted.

The weeks went by and with every clear test came a sense of renewed hope for my future and my family's future. Because I had such a rambunctious little boy at home, the days actually went by quite fast. I giggle when I think of how he was such a wild child. I know that a lot of people thought I didn't know how to "control" him. Maybe his way of being, our way of being, saved me. Maybe that's how I came out practically unscathed. In fact, I'm sure it is. Thank you Dustin!

Kim and I decided we would try again. We would try one more time. We had been through a lot and had survived. Though the past was difficult, it had made us stronger. We could try just one more time. We could get through anything now, couldn't we?

Back then the drug store pregnancy kits were expensive and unreliable, so at the first sign of pregnancy, I arranged an appointment with the doctor. The tests were positive! We were expecting again! My doctor was cautious, so he thought it best that I be placed under the care of a specialist. I was given some strict orders and some hormones as well. My joy was guarded, but all was going well. I was monitored frequently and felt really good about this pregnancy.

I would be so pleased when I looked at my swollen belly in the mirror. I would look at both profiles just to make sure I was getting bigger and that all was going smoothly. My mind would wander. I would ask myself: "I wonder if this is a girl?" Then I would quickly remind myself that the most important thing is that it is well. That it lives! My whole pregnancy was normal, other than one day that I had a migraine. I couldn't stand the light and lay in the dark basement all day. It eventually subsided, and my days went back to normal.

Oh no! Not again? I was about twenty five weeks into my pregnancy when I started cramping and having some bleeding. I rushed to the doctor hoping that he would tell me it was all for nothing. My fears shot through me. Was this punishment for hoping my baby was a girl? Would God do that? Would he be punishing me for not being grateful? My mind generated flurries of questions with no answers.

Okay, the bleeding had stopped, and it wasn't very much. The cramps were gone as well. I was trying to convince myself that everything was alright. He monitored the baby's heart rate, and surprisingly all was well. He convinced me to go home and take it easy. How was I to be super Mom if I had to take it easy? But I did take his advice.

Two weeks before the due date, our little girl, Jaisy Dai was born. She was healthy and was oh, so sweet! That was the happiest day of my life! I finally had what I thought to be a complete family.

Now that all was settled, I could continue to prove to everyone, but more importantly myself, that I was the best Mom ever.

When Jaisy Dai was three, due to lack of work, we decided to move. That move would take us eleven hours away from what we always knew as "home." We would be leaving our extended families as well as friends that we had known since grade school.

The new city was in a remote area, and the people I found were very materialistic and very private. Most people didn't give you the time of day; they were often working hard so they could buy the next best RV, vehicle or moving into a bigger home. It just seemed so cold.

Here I was, affirming that my surroundings were cold again. What I say and think comes right back to me. I found it hard to make friends, and I felt isolated.

Dustin was now in school and the demands of school were weighing heavy on me. His teachers – yes, his teachers – diagnosed him with Attention Deficit Disorder. Almost every day there was either a phone call from the school or a note sent home in his agenda complaining of his behavior. The principal even went as far as telling me, "Molly, you are a bad parent." How dare her! I was crushed at the time, but I now know she was just mirroring my insecurities. That and similar scenarios from the school enveloped me into a deep well of depression. I forever just wanted to prove that I could be a good Mom, the Best Mom, and here I was failing. I was failing at the only thing that I really wanted to succeed at.

My life came to a point that I couldn't find the will to get out of bed in the morning. I would get up, get the kids their breakfast. I would send Dustin off to school, and then I would go back to bed. Housework was done to necessity. Life itself hurt so much I couldn't imagine that the pain would ever go away. My emotions were so out of control. The only other emotions that I seemed to have were anger and frustration. I saw my life crashing down around me and most often, unless my children were around, I didn't care.

People were quick with platitudes such as "things will get better," "look at all that you have, " "there are a lot of people worse off than you," "pull yourself up by your bootstraps," "yes I know life isn't fair."

Thoughts of suicide crept in my head, but my mind always stopped me. I was fortunate enough not to be that deep into despair. I was able to keep myself "up" enough to think of my family and the grief they would go through. The best Mom ever could surely not commit suicide. Leaving my children motherless just wasn't an option.

My husband would pull me out of bed. Trying to engage me in exercise, he would literally take me by the hand, sometimes by the shoulders and lead me around the house or our yard. I laugh now because it was much like leading a cow around that got into the clover!

One day, as I was curled up on my bed in the fetal position, three-year-old Jaisy Dai crawled up and started stroking my hair. She always had a gentle side to her and was so wise for her age. She had/has the most loving hands…she is a true healer. I looked at her, really looked at her and started to think about what she was doing, what I was doing and what our future would be like if I stayed in bed. I sobbed while I hugged her, apologizing for how I was. I look back and think how pivotal that was, her coming to comfort me. Thank you, Jaisy Dai, for being in our lives and saving our family, and saving me.

When the tears were dried, I called my doctor's office for an appointment. The doctor had given me anti-depressants and referred me to a therapist. My therapy sessions were once a week, and they were life-saving. I was so thankful someone was there who knew what I was going through. My therapist was non-judgmental and with baby steps brought me bring me back to a functional state.

Healing has been a process. I was not satisfied with just a "functional" state, so I continued researching as to what I could do for myself. This led me to researching and embracing spirituality and the connection between the mind, body, and the spirit.

I was aware I was on a spiritual path about seven years ago. It has made such a profound difference in my life. At the start I kept it quiet, in a spiritual closet so to speak. I wasn't very open to my husband, family, friends and certainly not to my coworkers. I worked with a variety of caregivers of a certain nature and most, if not all, were trained that conventional type medicine, psychiatry or psychotherapy were the way to treat any diseases, anxieties or mental illnesses.

I started going to workshops and talking to like-minded people. I read several books. My first books were that of Louise L. Hay, Wayne Dyer, Masaru Emoto, Don Miguel Ruiz and Neale Donald Walsch. They have truly been a saving grace. Since then I've added a repertoire of Cheryl Richardson, Marianne Williams, Bruce Lipton, Caroline Myss, Joan Z. Borysenko and many more.

> **❝** The spiritual path – is simply
>
> the journey of living our lives.
>
> Everyone is on a spiritual path;
>
> most people just don't know it. **❞**
>
> ~ *Marianne Williamson*

I will share some of my beliefs and practices. Please keep in mind that I am a work in progress. My belief system is that we get back what we put out there, or what we think we deserve. I believe that everything that we say and think is supported by the Universe. We choose our destiny before we are born and that we are reincarnated. I believe we're here on this earth to learn and grow. We choose how we come into this life based on what "lessons" we have to learn. We all have lessons. Some people seem to have harder ones than others. Those lessons challenge and guide us to find meaning and understanding behind them, thus opening us up to the awareness of ourselves and Spirit, which is one and the same.

Some of my practices are:

• Above all, Self Love; Love is a miracle cure. Self Love has made the biggest difference in my life. I am achieving this through mirror work, which Louise L. Hay, author of *You Can Heal Your Life*, is a huge proponent of. It has been the foundation of my healing. I don't ever pass a mirror without telling myself, "I love you." Learning to love myself has definitely been the turning point in my road to living an authentic life.

• I have embraced an attitude of gratitude. I give thanks before I get out of bed in the morning and before I fall asleep at night. I bless my meals, special occasions and anything that spontaneously arises during the course of the day.

> **66** Gratitude unlocks the fullness of life.
>
> It turns what we have into enough, and more.
>
> It turns denial into acceptance, chaos to order,
>
> confusion to clarity.
>
> It can turn a meal into a feast, a house into a home,
>
> a stranger into a friend.
>
> Gratitude makes sense of our past, brings peace
>
> for today, and creates a vision for tomorrow **99**
>
> ~ *Melody Beattie*

• Laughter is good medicine. It provides a physical and emotional release. I enjoy being silly. As my family will attest; no one in this world enjoys my jokes, my humor, as much as I do. I like to surround myself with people who have a good sense of humor.

Studies have shown that laughter reduces the level of stress hormones. It also increases the level of health-enhancing hormones. It produces a stronger immune system, as well as fewer physical effects of stress. A good belly laugh exercises the diaphragm, contracts the abdominal muscles and even works out the shoulders, leaving muscles more relaxed afterward. It will also provide a good workout for the heart. Laughter brings the focus away from anger, guilt, stress and negative emotions in a more beneficial way than other mere distractions.

Laughter connects us with others. Just as with smiling and kindness, most people find that laughter is contagious. By elevating the mood of those around you, you can reduce their stress levels, and perhaps improve the quality of social interaction you experience with them, reducing your stress level even more!

• I maintain a daily meditation. In most meditations you want to quiet the mind. This requires the skills of concentration that develops over time. I also practice guided and visual meditation.

There are several ways to meditate. Some might consider a walk in nature to be a meditation.

Deepak Chopra practices Primordial Sound Meditation. He estimates that people who meditate for many years often have a biological age that is between 5 and 10 years lower than their chronological age. It has an immense positive effect on the three great indicators of aging: our sense of hearing, our blood pressure and our eyesight.

Meditation can help those with conditions caused by or exacerbated by psychological stress.

As a stress reducer, it is effective in reducing high blood pressure, chronic pain and insomnia.

Hormones with a calming effect like melatonin and serotonin increase as a result of meditating, whereas the stress hormone cortisol decreases.

• I keep a positive outlook by staying grounded and by meditating. If a negative thought comes into my consciousness, I gently tell it to pass by and replace it with the opposite of what it was.

> 66 There are two kinds of mystics in the world –
> the optimystics, and the pessimystics.
> The pessimystics are telling us, 'The sky is falling!'
> The optimystics say, 'No, it only looks that way
> because we are ascending.' 99
> ~ Swami Beyondananda

• I practice affirmations. Affirmations are anything you say or think. Whether you know it or not you're affirming and creating your life with every thought and every word. I take time to consciously choose words that will create positive situations in my life. As Louise L. Hay writes in her book, Experience Your Good Now, "It's a beginning point on the path to change."

66 There is no such thing as an idle thought.

All thought creates form on some level.

Every thought leads to either love or fear. **99**

~ A Course in Miracles

- Forgiveness begins the healing process. I chose to release the past and forgive. I found it hardest to forgive myself, but I did and now I can move on.

66 To forgive is to set a prisoner free

and discover that the prisoner was you. **99**

~ Lewis B. Smedes

- I don't take anything personally. This is not easy to do, until you realize that when you take it personally you are agreeing with what they said or what they did. Whatever you think and whatever you feel is your problem. Nothing other people do is because of you. It is because of themselves.

66 That which offends you, weakens you. **99**

~ Wayne Dyer

I have shared just a few of my practices with you. They have been very effective for my life, but each person has to listen to their intuition to find what resonates with them. When a person finds something that makes so much sense and has made such a positive impact on their life, it is hard to keep it to themselves. It is hard to resist the temptation to go on an all out crusade to heal everyone whether they want it or not.

I knew through my mentors, what I had read, and what I had experienced, that if I wanted the special people in my world to experience this incredible life that I am now living, I couldn't dump this on them. What is necessary is that I continue to grow. I would be what I wanted them to be. I would have to keep in mind:

66 You must be the change you want to see in the world. **99**

~ Mahatma Gandhi

I had long waited for Hay House to showcase their "I Can Do It!" Conference in Western Canada. I had always wanted to go to one but was reluctant to pay for the flights to Toronto or to the States. The time had come: It would be held in Vancouver in March! While talking to my son, who now lives in Vancouver, I was excited to tell him I would be coming to visit him.

It came as a big surprise when he said that he wanted to join me at the conference. He had always been supportive of my spiritual ventures, but I really didn't think he would be interested in them. That night I told my husband of the news of Dustin taking in the conference. He, too, said he would like to come. Then I told Jaisy Dai, and she also said that she wanted to attend. So it will be a family affair.

I am so happy for myself and my family and truly proud of their quest to live their best life. I always wanted what was best for my family. I wanted to be the Best Mom Ever! I have come to the realization that I did the best I could with the knowledge and support I had at the time…. Certainly not unlike my Mother did!

66 May the long time sun shine upon you,

may all love surround you

and the pure light within you

guide your way on. 99

~ Celtic Blessing

KIMBERLY S. PRATTE

Chapter 5:

Healing Through Forgiveness

CHAPTER 5
Healing Through Forgiveness

My purpose is to share with you my journey towards self-awareness and healing through forgiveness. I first needed to learn how to forgive myself and eliminate negative self-esteem beliefs in order to begin the process of changing my mind and reprogramming my subconscious. Believe me, this started with BABY steps! This "paradigm shift" was only possible because I was able to visualize it, understand it, and was determined to reach it and completely remember it. Ultimately, this has led to a sense of well-being, a state of wellness, in every aspect of my life like I have never experienced before.

The irony is I'm actually a very strong person. I have endured the worst of situations and have come out on the other side. I may have been scathed, but I never gave up. I kept trying to find a better way, only I was lacking the tools I needed to truly make this change become my reality. I went through the whole "I'm angry at God thing," asking myself "why is God allowing this to happen?" PERHAPS YOU ARE FEELING THE SAME WAY.

My goal is to help others who have been abused. But up until now I didn't know how, especially since I couldn't seem to get my own life straight. I was entrenched in a cycle of being abused. At the time I didn't realize I was allowing the abuse, and enabling these people by making excuses for them. All I wanted was to have a healthy relationship and raise a family. I had so much love in my heart and so much love to give. I also happened to be a very forgiving and patient person. While these are very good qualities to have, I didn't know how to care for myself, or how to set healthy boundaries.

I want to share my story with those seeking a life of purpose, peace, and love. The core of which is gratitude for everything you have, and realizing you are an amazing person created with a divine purpose in this world. You may find yourself asking "why do these things keep happening to me?" Well, it begins with you. It's easier to blame others instead of looking into yourself and recognizing that you are responsible for what's happening to you. That's a hard thing to turn around.

You need to reframe the way you view life in general and as a whole. This encompasses everything in the world around you, the way you react to others, and the way you view others' reactions to you. You need to reframe your thoughts and change the way you look at everything.

I'm not saying you deserve to be abused, or that you asked for it. No one deserves to be mistreated in ANY way. When I say you are responsible for what's happening to you, it's because you aren't doing anything to stop it. You don't know what you don't know, therefore you cannot make a change because you do not understand the change has to begin within you.

Life had beaten me down to a point where I truly believed that I didn't matter, and that no one would ever really love me. I always made sure everyone else was happy and didn't attend to my own real needs. I was frozen in this reality creating negative energy within and around myself. I didn't allow myself to be my natural self, causing my life to be a much more unpleasant experience than what it really was, or should have been. I was grateful for my life, my health, my family, my job, and especially took great pleasure and pride in my children, who I adore. But I was always looking to the outside for things to make me happy. Instead, while addressing my needs, I should have been looking within and having gratitude for who I am and my own uniqueness.

You cannot be strong for others if you are not strong for yourself. I had to stop looking at what everyone else was doing, and look inward to see what was going on inside of me, causing me to allow things in my life that do not serve me. What are my triggers? How can I change what I'm attracting into my life?

> 66 You cannot be strong for others if
> you are not strong for yourself. 99
> ~ *Patricia Pratte*

My pattern started developing when I was very young and my father left us. I was just 2-1/2 years old and my brother was 5. Our father had nothing to do with us, nor did he make sure we were provided for and had the things we needed. He completely abandoned our family from that point on.

At first mom kept us with her, and had a babysitter come during the day so she could work in order to provide for us. The babysitter didn't work out and this is where our separation from mom began. My brother and I spent the weekdays at our grandparents' farm, only to see and be with mom on the weekends.

Grandpa quickly became my father figure, I trusted him to always be there for me. He took care of me and made sure I had the things I needed. There

Restoring Your Beautiful Life

was a flip-side to staying with grandma and grandpa though, interwoven with the happy times and memories are sad memories, even scary memories, of grandma and grandpa's terrible arguments. This impacted how I viewed relationships and what was acceptable behavior.

At the age of five, I was very excited to be getting my own real dad. Mom was marrying a wonderful man who I adored not only then, but do to this day. My mother soon became pregnant, I couldn't believe my good fortune to be getting a baby of our own to love and enjoy. But not long after my brother was born is when another shift took place for me. I felt displaced by my little brother and again felt as if someone was taking my mother away from me. But, there was an even bigger change that has taken most of my life to overcome.

Late one evening when my younger brother was 6 months old we got a phone call. It was someone calling to let my mother know grandpa had intentionally and purposefully ended his life. My world was shattered. Being young I didn't understand suicide, I just knew he had died. I felt so alone, so betrayed, so abandoned. I remember thinking to myself, how could he leave me, why didn't he want to stay with me, was I such a bad girl to be such a disappointment to him that he didn't want to be with me, didn't he know how much I loved him, how unfair, how much I was counting on him and trusting him to be there with me always, now he was gone. I was too young to realize there was something much bigger within him that he could not handle, and it had nothing to do with me. It's amazing how this impacted my life.

For many years after this, I remember thinking to myself, "everyone I love will just leave me." At the same time I was desperate for people to love me. What a sad way to feel. I had very low self-esteem and felt unworthy of love. This has affected every relationship in my life since. At a young age I began forming the thought pattern that if I take care of someone and selflessly give of myself by doing things to help them with all of their needs, then I will surely be loved. It was disappointing when my needs weren't met.

Growing up I didn't learn to acknowledge my own feelings or needs. Instead, I always worried about everyone else and how they were feeling. I never really took myself into consideration. I was a pleaser, a peacemaker. I learned this from my experiences as a young girl, combined with how I witnessed my mother unselfishly giving of herself to care for others in the family, especially grandma after grandpa passed away.

This is an admirable quality that needs to be balanced with boundaries, self-care, respect and love for yourself. In the words of my mom as we discussed my section of this book, "You have to be strong in yourself in order to be strong for others." What a great message.

I became a rescuer, to the point of allowing myself to be a victim. I didn't have boundaries, or the realization of my boundaries and what was acceptable behavior towards me. I made excuses for others and just wanted to be loved back. I couldn't understand why others treated me with such disrespect, when all I did was respect, fully support, and love them. In other words, I let people walk all over me by allowing myself to be a doormat.

This is the perfect scenario, an unknowing invitation for abusive people to come into your life and overpower you before you even realize what is happening. Wow! Was THAT ever a difficult realization to come to and accept. I've had to change my entire way of thinking about myself and the relationships with everyone in my life from co-workers, to friends, to acquaintances and my entire family. I am just as important as everyone else, and yes, my needs are just as important.

My first marriage began at the age of 18 and lasted for 16 years. The product of that relationship is my four beautiful children of whom I'm extremely proud. My desire in life was to have a home, and to be a good wife and mother. I wasn't career driven, and I didn't finish college. But after sixteen years I knew I could no longer stay in that relationship. The reasons began weeks after we married, with him becoming very controlling, in addition to emotionally and physically abusive. Soon after we married I became pregnant, and he used our child as a pawn to keep me with him. He made threats that if I left him, he would take our child away from me as soon as he was born, and I would never see him again. He would throw me across the room, and slam me against the wall in order to get his point across, and he also drank excessively. I was young and very naive, therefore his scare tactics and threats were very effective. I was miserable, and did not know what to do.

When I was six months' pregnant with our first child, he and his parents loaded up all of my things and drove me to my parents' house. They threw all of my things out in the driveway and left me standing there.

He had just decided he didn't want to be married, filed for divorce and custody of our child as soon as he was born. His parents then took him on a two-week vacation to Florida. He came back into the picture one month before the baby was born, with statements of regret and promises of how he would behave in the future. He swore he would never hit me, or abuse me in any way, ever again. However, it didn't take long for that promise to be broken.

I stayed in the marriage, and we had three more children. The abuse continued, and really escalated when he finished college and became an officer in the Army. He had a drinking problem, and severe anger control issues which had only worsened.

I was terrified to get divorced. Having never lived on my own and taken care of myself, I didn't feel I was equipped to deal with the situation. I didn't want my children to become latch-key kids and not have a father. But, staying in the marriage was not an option either. It was hurting me on every level, and I had lost complete sight of who I was. I'm hoping to give you some of the tools you might need in order to deal with your own situation, and better understand yourself.

I made the huge mistake of agreeing to split custody of our four children, and trusted him when he said I could see the kids whenever I wanted. The visitation order was never followed by him, yet I always made sure he had the kids when it was his time. After the divorce, I had been struggling to make ends meet. I was not receiving child support or alimony. We were on food stamps for awhile, and I didn't eat until after my children were finished eating. I became very thin. Having no degree, and no real work experience, I felt as if I could not provide enough for my children and didn't know how we were going to make it.

I moved to Wisconsin and eventually met a man who would became my husband. He was extremely cruel, and I became TERRIFIED of him. He was an ex-marine who combined extremely emotionally abusive tactics with physical threats. After six months of marriage I moved out, but out of extreme fear did not file for divorce until three years later.

He stole precious and very sentimental things from me, threw away family belongings, stripped me of my car and cost me a lot of money, in addition to further tearing apart my family. He didn't want us to have anything more than what he gave to us. He tried to strip away our entire past, and all of the things that were important to us.

I was in the midst of a child support battle with my children's father and was trying to get custody of my other two sons. My then-husband was so vindictive, he vowed if I tried to divorce him, he would team up with my first husband to make sure I never saw or heard from my kids again.

This battle went on for almost five years and ended with the children's father being awarded continued custody of the two boys. The judge stated: *"Why should this man be punished for being a soldier defending his country?"* If only the judge knew what was really going on.

A few months later I went to pick up my youngest son for a visitation and had a letter thrown in my face by the step-mom as she stated: "Read it." I told her I didn't want to read anything she had written, but she promised me I would. I read it to discover it was a letter stating that this was not a visitation, but a permanent change of residency.

I was shocked for many reasons. First of all, what was the whole court battle for? Why didn't they just let me have custody of my sons in the first place? And, this change of residency was only for my youngest son, not his older brother. My youngest son knew nothing of this, she had packed his bag with only the things she wanted him to have from the house. He only had two changes of clothes as if it was for the weekend, and his paintball gun which she broke for him when she packed it.

Find your strength to walk away from whatever situation is demeaning you or causing you grief, no matter how hard it may seem. I kept making the same bad choices in who I allowed into my life, and then couldn't understand why these abusive men seemed attracted to me. I now know that it was because I unknowingly presented myself as a victim and weak; they saw me coming from a mile away.

I have learned self-love and responsibility through discovering and acknowledging what my real needs are, and by not living for everyone else and their happiness. Addressing my needs and meeting them. Realizing I don't have to please everyone else, or worry what others think about my thoughts, feelings, or ideas. No one knows me better than I know myself. I've been told how strong I am ... that isn't always a good thing, especially when you don't have clear boundaries set for yourself. Life isn't an endurance test. Sometimes you need to be weak and cared for, it's really okay and healthy. But this doesn't necessarily mean by someone else, rather first and foremost by you taking care of yourself and meeting your own needs. It's exhausting always taking care of everyone else and their needs and not having your own met.

Do you identify with this? Do you have a hard time saying no, no matter how difficult it may make things for you? Are you constantly selflessly going out of your way to please or help others, without reciprocation?

When I finally filed for divorce from my last husband, I met a man who was very different from my usual dating choice. He was interested not only in my health and well-being, but truly the welfare of all of my children, and in helping all of us to rise above the abuse. He truly wants us to be healthy, happy, and no longer be victims. He has done nothing but encourage me to become the person God intended me to be. He was just what I needed, when I needed it. This is where the real transformation began.

&ぺ Restoring Your Beautiful Life

I was ready to make the changes, and do the work necessary to get the other side. Being finally free, I vowed to never go back into an abusive situation. I was no longer going to allow myself to be a victim. Enough!! Negative energy, attracts negativity, I was ready to turn it into positive energy.

Negative energy, attracts negativity.

I'm not going to go into much detail about specific relationships and the issues of abuse that followed, since that is not my goal. I'm simply taking away the lessons, forgiving and learning self-love and responsibility. Through this process, I'm finding my voice and learning how to express my feelings, wants, and needs while standing in the truth of who I am. I need to be connected to myself, in order to truly be connected to others.

I needed to stop living a lie and seek the truth, to find my way and soar like an eagle. It began with learning how to forgive myself, and how to nurture myself.

I've had to learn I could not control the way someone treated or responded to me, but I am in control of the way I choose to respond. Others do not make me angry, I allow myself to become angry. Therefore I need to take a look inside of myself and see what is causing my emotion, what is triggering me. With skills I've now acquired I am able to more clearly see and feel what is real, and appropriately address my needs. If I would have had these tools a long time ago, I would not have chosen to allow these people into my life.

There comes a point when you get tired of rescuing everyone else, and trying to fix everything for them. It isn't giving up, it's realizing you don't need to allow certain people to suck the life out of you. As you begin to change, the people you attract into your life will change. Some people will not like the changes, and others will be delighted. Let the ones go who are not supportive of the new and improved you, as they no longer serve you. Surround yourself with like-minded people who lovingly support and inspire one another to grow and dream.

This is when I met a man who has given me and my children a great deal of support in our journey towards healing and forgiveness. Through a friend of his, we have made a connection with an amazing man named Jim Morningstar. Jim is the founder and director of Transformations USA and the School of Integrative Psychology in Milwaukee, Wisconsin. I'm currently a second-year student in his school.

It truly is life-changing work which enables you to transform your life from fear and suffering to love and inner peace, if you are ready to learn the tools and make the changes necessary. It's a lot of work, and at times extremely difficult to transform your way of processing your thoughts and reacting to situations. A large part of the work was to peel away the layers that built up over the years, and getting back to the core of who I really am by letting go of what no longer serves me. That would be all of the hurt, disappointment, regret, and feelings of abandonment.

It has been a long journey of self-discovery and reconnecting with myself in order to find out what is really important to me and what I want. I had to learn how to stop running and get back to my truth, the truth of who I really am. I've always lived for everyone else.

The journey hasn't been easy. There have been times when I have gone backwards, but then I'll take great strides forward. I'm a work in progress. We are always evolving, learning, changing, and growing – we never stay the same. Now I'm on a path of joy, abundance, gratitude, and truly knowing who I am. I realize what my purpose is and intent on fulfilling it.

Let go of life's hurts, disappointments and regrets. These things no longer serve you, but rather inhibit your growth and cloud your vision. When we hold onto these things, they build layers around us. It's amazing the difference once we let go of attachments and negativity. I'm living proof of this! My life is taking directions I once thought I could only dream about. I'm attracting what I'm putting out.

Be mindful of your thoughts and words, choose them wisely. When you are negative, you attract negativity. Face your fears head on. Break the barriers you have built for yourself, and tear down the walls. Only you can free yourself, resolve to evolve. Practice thinking positive and uplifting thoughts, then enjoy the journey.

Holding onto our past inhibits our growth and keeps us from our full potential. Don't be defined by your past, instead define your future. We truly are like onions, peel away all of the junk in those layers and get back to the core of who you really are. Shed the image you have of yourself and have fun recreating who you are. Start celebrating you by acknowledging yourself for the strength you have, and the beautiful person you are.

Human nature is to hold on to past hurts. Things have happened to all of us – be it past mistakes, or being hurt by someone. We tend to define ourselves by our story. This is a very difficult thing to turn around. You need to start looking at yourself in a different way.

The first step is to begin reframing your thoughts with doing daily affirmations. At first these affirmations are going to seem really stupid, and you'll try to talk yourself out of it by saying: "This will never work." But with consistency and repetition of telling yourself you are worthy, you are loved, you are deserving, you are beautiful, you are of value, you are provided for and you're perfect just the way you are, you will begin to change.

I know you've heard it said, "God doesn't make mistakes!" Well, He doesn't. Standing in the mirror and looking into your own eyes as you say these affirmations to yourself, adds to the impact – it's very powerful. This will be very hard to do when you first begin the process, you may feel like they are only words you are saying, and they don't have any meaning for you. You won't believe the words you are saying to yourself to be true. After some time and sticking with it, you will start to reframe the way you look at yourself and start believing what you are telling yourself. Your thoughts will turn around because what you're saying is true. You are worthy, you are loved, everybody here on this planet is worthy and beautiful in their own way. Some people just have more lessons to learn, or more things to figure out.

Another helpful, healing tool is called positive mirroring. Select the words you want to more deeply insert into your consciousness. Then have someone "mirror" them back to you. For example: I would say to you, "You are loved and cared for." Then you would say back to me "I am loved and cared for." Repeat this back and forth several times and play with it. Say it strong and loud with much meaning, then whisper it in each ear, yell it at the top of your lungs. Have fun!

By utilizing a tool called couples communication, I have greatly enhanced the conversations I have with my loved ones. Couples communication is really quite simple, yet when you are on a sensitive subject it is very difficult to do. With time it gets easier. It goes like this.

You and your partner pick who will be "A" and who will be "B." When it is "A's" turn they state, "What I'm feeling is......."; next they state, "What I need from you is...."; and lastly, "What I'm willing to do is.....".
Then when it's "B's" turn they respond, "What I hear you saying is...";
then, "How that makes me feel is...."; and lastly, "What I'm willing to do is...".

Keep taking turns until you work through the issue and the air is clear. We all have themes in our lives, and you can get stuck. For me there had been an underlying theme of abandonment, and a theme of lack – there not being enough for me. I hoped that maybe someday it would be my turn. These are all scripts I've repeated over and over in my head my whole life. I felt as if I was inadequate and missing out on something. I didn't feel complete.

My nature is to always find the silver lining, seeing the good in people and in every situation. In the past I have gone over and above to do more and give more of myself in the hopes of everything working out fine. I tried to make everyone else around me feel loved and needed, all the while feeling unloved, unsupported, and unwanted myself. I kept promising myself: "It will get better" – but it never did.

That's because I wasn't taking care of me, I wasn't setting boundaries. I was allowing others to disrespect me. I had to learn how to rewrite those scripts in order to reframe my beliefs about myself so that I could begin living a life of gratitude and abundance.

Key components to your spiritual growth and development are integrating your mind, body, and spirit to find your purpose. Your mind, body and spirit are all connected, you cannot neglect one and expect the other parts to be healthy and happy. It's important to not only take care of the mental aspects, but also focus on the body. Stress depletes you of necessary nutrients and manifests illness. By changing my diet and starting a vitamin regimen, getting more rest, exercising, and learning how to nurture myself, I have a sense of balance and wholeness.

For example, I had developed severe chronic pain and became hypothyroid. After discovering I had a severe Vitamin D deficiency, I started taking vitamin supplements as well as making better choices with my foods. I now avoid processed food and eating out whenever possible, and have decreased my intake of caffeine. I choose organic fresh fruits and vegetables, eat less red meat and fat, and eat more whole grains. All of these changes combined have made a huge impact on my life for the better. I have started to get some of my energy back, I sleep better, and hardly have any pain left.

Take time out for quiet mediation. Spend time experiencing your thoughts and feelings. Notice them, allowing the thoughts to come into your mind, and feel the feeling in your body. Acknowledge them and release them without judgment. We need to stop placing judgments on everything. Stop judging our emotions, our anger, our sadness, our fear. Don't judge your happiness, just let it be what it is and learn how to appreciate each emotion, acknowledging it and letting it go, don't hold onto it.

I've learned how to appreciate my emotions and how to stay with them and feel them, acknowledging them and letting them go. It's okay to be mad, sad, glad, and feel good about it as long as you find healthy ways of expressing your emotions and also have the voice to express them and feel safe. A lot of my frustration came from not knowing how to amply express what I was feeling and get my point across in an manner that relayed my truth to the other person. I was so used to not being heard, or told what I was thinking and/or feeling.

Think about all of the tools of distraction we use so we don't have to think or feel. Distractions keep us from truly being in tune with who we are and what we really want. We use things such as drugs, alcohol, sex, TV, going out with friends, electronics, or listening to music. We don't allow ourselves to simply sit quietly and listen to our hearts, what we want, need, feel, or know. We need to reconnect and check in with ourselves daily, that is part of staying balanced.

There is no such thing as a mistake, merely opportunities to learn and grow.

Issues from the past prevent us from experiencing success. Don't focus on the past and dwell on the negative, move forward and find gratitude in your heart and live a grateful life. It really does not only turn around the way you view yourself and your life, but you attract the things you want in your life and your relationships improve.

The people that no longer serve your highest good, will disappear from your life and you will attract healthier relationships. It's amazing the power in positive thinking, just as much as negativity has an impact. You can make a choice to dwell in the negative, or even in the most adverse conditions focus on the positives and find gratitude, pulling on your strengths and care for yourself as you move forward.

There is no such thing as a mistake, merely opportunities to learn and grow.

I recently attended an "Enlightenment Intensive," and during the entire weekend we didn't have any distractions such as telephones, TV, or music, and we ate a very healthy balanced diet. Everything was taken care of for us so that we could be as free as children. This enabled us to focus on "who we are" with no worries of time frames and duties. We weren't even supposed to talk unless we were talking about "who we are." We needed to just be in our heads in order to get past our "story." I came away from the weekend with a brand new lease on life, and now have a completely different opinion of myself. I choose to no longer be defined by my past.

Our experiences can be used for healing. Everything I've done in my life so far has led me to this point. I would not be a co-author of this book if I had not had the life experiences I've had.

Life doesn't have to be a struggle, it should be joyous and happy. It doesn't matter how much or little you have in material things; it does matter what you hold inside, and how you feel about yourself and the world you live in. Is it a safe place where all of your needs are provided for? Ironically, I find I'm happier with less material things. To me this equals less stress, and less drama. I don't have a need to keep up with the Joneses, I would rather focus on what makes me happy, and helping others achieve happiness.

Learn to pay attention to your body and the messages it's giving you. For example, if your throat is getting tight, your heart starts beating fast, or you notice a funny feeling in your stomach, then your body is telling you something isn't right. When you're in the midst of trauma, or you're being abused, your frame of mind doesn't allow you to pay attention to the warnings your body is giving you. You may feel the fear, but you're not addressing what really is going on and confronting what you need to do in order to take care of yourself.

Breathing is important to your well-being because it nurtures every part of your body with the oxygen it needs. When we aren't breathing properly, our body gets out of balance. Breathing is also a very efficient tool for releasing stress. When you begin to feel stressed, or a tightness in your chest, close your eyes and take a few slow, deep breaths.

Take time out during the day to pay attention to how you are breathing. It's a good way to check in with yourself and notice what you are feeling – whether it is anxious, scared, relaxed, happy or mad. You will be amazed the difference it makes to merely change your breath.

What nourishes you? Is it spending time sitting in silence, walking in nature, spending time with loved ones, supporting a friend, a bubble bath, writing? Whatever it may be, create a list for yourself and note when you last did the things you listed. Read your list and resolve to do one of the things on your list today and choose one thing to do the next day. Start taking time out each day to nurture yourself.

I encourage you to learn self-love and how to nurture yourself, as well as forgiveness and acceptance. Feel good about your feelings and find healthy ways of expressing them. That's where a lot of my frustration came from. I didn't know how to amply express what I was feeling partly because I was so used to not being heard. I used to get frustrated and yell in order to be heard, and even then I was not heard.

A few weeks ago my daughter told me how proud she is of me. At first I didn't know how to respond. She was acknowledging the changes I have made, and recognizing the differences in my life. Over the past year all of my children and others in my life have acknowledged the changes I have made. YOU CAN DO IT, TOO.

Let go of what no longer serves you and stand in your power. Things may not always turn out the way we want them to, just remember in the end everything happens for a reason. We are given choices and face difficult situations. Be capable of remaining in your truth no matter what the situation is.

Value yourself for who you are, not what you do. Know that you are taken care of and trust in that. The thoughts you hold in your conscious mind become your reality. THINK POSITIVE! Never stop thinking about your dreams and goals. Visualize them and take steps to make them happen. I look forward to living the rest of my life knowing and speaking my truth; I have found my voice. Have you found yours?

SHELLY YORK

Chapter 6:

A Spoon In the Road

CHAPTER 6
A Spoon In the Road

My story isn't all that uncommon. Many of us have married, had children and divorced. And most of us have carried secrets deep within our souls and lied to ourselves over and over until we couldn't look at ourselves in the mirror anymore.

Months before I ever met Mike, I had gone to a psychic fair. The psychic that I met that day told me that I was soon going to meet a man who worked in construction, and that he would be wearing some sort of funny boots.

That psychic was spot on with her prediction. Mike and I actually met on Halloween night in 1997at a nightclub. I was dressed as a French maid, and he was dressed as a fisherman wearing wading boots and carrying a small fishing pole. I was there with some close friends and their boyfriends. One of the boyfriends, Rudy, played softball with Mike, and that is how we became introduced.

We chatted, drank and danced for most of the night but when it came time to leave, we, for whatever reason, did not exchange phone numbers. But, he did invite me to come out and watch him play softball. I didn't show up to a game until three weeks later – talk about playing hard to get, ha!

Once I did finally decide to go to a game, Mike didn't waste any time in asking me out for the following night, and that is how we became Mike and Shelly – the couple. We became joined at the hip from that moment forward. As with all new romantic beginnings, it was a magical time. Looking back, even though I was 25 when I met Mike, I was really still just a young, naïve girl. A girl who thought that she was finally ready to play grown-up. If I am to be extremely honest, I would have to admit that I was…lonely and envious of my friends. My closest friends all had boyfriends and were part of a "relationship." I was the 5th wheel, the odd one out.

I wanted very much to be in a relationship – to be loved and cherished by somebody special. Oh, how I dreamed that I would meet my Prince Charming. And, then along came Mike. He treated me unlike any other man ever had. He was always showering me with compliments, affection, flowers and was always surprising me with something special. I wasn't used to being treated like this, the way a lady really should be treated. Pretty sad, huh?

I remember when Mike first told me that he loved me. I was like a deer frozen in the headlights, my brain went numb, and when I did speak all I said was "thank you." I had already been questioning the depth of my feelings, and I knew that he cared a great deal more about me than I did for him. He was filling a void in my heart and in my life. He had become my absolute best friend very quickly.

We shared everything with one another – everything but the real truth...the truth about how I truly felt about him. I wasn't "in love" with him. At least not in a romantic sense. I loved him as my best friend. But one thing that I was certain of, was that I was not willing to hurt or lose him.

So, a little more time passed, and we started talking about marriage. At this point, I had already said those three HUGE words to him: *I love you.* I just never clarified what kind of love I truly felt. Our relationship was moving quickly, and I will admit that I was definitely getting caught up in all the excitement of the possibility of being a bride.

And then it happened. Mike officially proposed to me on March 31, 1998. I was thrilled, excited and overjoyed. I remember us going over to tell my parents and show them my beautiful engagement ring. We then went out to dinner, and I played my part as the glowing bride-to-be. I let myself get caught up in the fantasy of being "in love," being loved and engaged. What girl doesn't dream of these moments? My head was definitely up in the clouds, and I got carried away with living in this fantasy world that Mike and I were in.

And, then there was his family. They were everything that my family was not. His parents worked together in their family-owned business. My Dad had worked for the same printing company for as long as I can remember (not saying that there is anything wrong with that) and my Mom was a homemaker. His parents often traveled to Las Vegas for golf tournaments and pleasure. My family would detour through Vegas on our way home from my Grandparents' place every summer while returning from our family vacation. Mike's family lived in a big, beautiful home. My family lived in a cute and cozy 1,000 sq. ft. home. Mike and I simply came from extremely different backgrounds, and I was more than excited to explore his way of living.

So, we started planning our wedding for May of 1999, and it was fun. During this time though, I started pulling away from Mike physically and looking back I can see how I started to become emotionally distant and unavailable as well. Mike was always telling me that we should go to Vegas and elope. My response was always: *"Hell no! I'm not getting married in Vegas!"*

Restoring Your Beautiful Life

During this time , Mike had come home one day and told me that I never surprised him anymore. I'm not quite sure how I came up with the idea, but I soon decided to throw a surprise wedding. We were already going on a family trip to Vegas in July to celebrate his sister's birthday, so why not add an element of surprise to this trip? So, I spoke with his parents about the idea and together we hatched a plan.

We flew into Vegas on a Thursday. Mike bought into the idea that a lot of his family from out of state were there as a mini-family reunion and to celebrate his sister's 21st birthday. I remember everything being so chaotic. I had to give our guests instructions to check into the hotel during specific hours, and I had to make sure that Mike and I were away from the hotel and casino as much as possible to ensure that we didn't bump into any of our friends or family. It was absolutely crazy!! But fabulous and exciting at the same time.

So, on Thursday night, we went out and had a big family dinner for his sister's birthday. Then on Friday night, as we were walking over to his parent's room, we ran into (purposely planned) his Dad who was standing in one of the corridors. His Dad linked arms with us and guided us into a reception hall which was filled with about 75 of our friends and family. Mike, of course, had no clue what was going on. I took his hand and led him to a chair. I then sat in his lap and whispered into his ear "Will you marry me tomorrow?" He, of course, said "Yes!" I had already planned the whole wedding and taken care of all the details. Pretty much, all he had to do was show up and say *"I do."*

That Saturday, July 11, 1998, I remember standing outside the double doors that led into the reception hall where I was to be married. I was shaking like a leaf and hyperventilating into a brown paper bag. It was truly like watching a scene out of a movie. My Dad said, "Shelly, it's not too late. You don't have to go through with this if you don't want to." All I could see in my head was dollar signs and a broken-hearted Mike. My parents had paid so much for this wedding, and Mike was already waiting at the altar for me. I had to go thru with it. There was no backing out NOW, I said to myself as the music began and the doors opened. Down the aisle I went to become Mrs. Michael York.

We met on Halloween night in 1997, starting dating a few days before Thanksgiving, were engaged on March 31st and married on July 11, 1998. Roughly, we knew each other for about 8 months before getting married. Looking back, I now know that if I would have kept to my original wedding plans, I never would have gone through with it, but because I was afraid of breaking this beautiful man's heart, I did something so crazy as to have a surprise wedding and to move our wedding date up almost a year from when we had it planned for. Instead of breaking his heart, I broke my own and self – sacrificed any possibility of true love or passion for myself. Very soon after our marriage, I began to change. I didn't realize it at the time, but looking back, I can see how I became emotionally distant from not only Mike but to everyone that I knew. Inside of me a raging war was going on. There was a lot of anger and resentment toward myself for being a coward and marrying a man that I truly did not love the way that you should when you marry someone. Choosing to marry Mike was my fork in the road, and I felt that I had chosen the wrong path.

I'm sure that it was because of many things, including my emotional distance and just the way that Mike was wired, but he became a very difficult and negative person to live with. He had been this way already for a few years but by this point, it was really starting to chip away at me. I felt as though I was always walking on pins and needles. It felt like he was always yelling at me through his body language. I began to withdraw from him more. It was just easier and more pleasant to live inside my head. The years passed quickly. We bought our first home in August of 2002, and before we knew it, we had our daughter in February of 2003. Our life looked really great to outsiders. But really, very little was good. Mike and I were embarking on some of the most troubling years of our lives, and we had no clue.

In short:

Early in 2003, Mike got injured on the job and after a surgery on his arm; he was no longer able to return to his former profession as an Electrician, and we began to have financial problems. From summer of 2003 to January of 2004, I lost two Grandparents and Mike lost one of his grandmothers. My Grandma on my Mom's side of the family had been sick for a while so it wasn't a surprise when she passed, but when my Grandpa on my Dad's side of the family took his own life, it absolutely devastated the family. Due to our financial struggles, we made the decision to move to North Texas in January 2005. Mike became involved in the clean-up of Hurricane Katrina, invested tons of money in equipment, a truck and a travel trailer and literally overnight, we were about $120,000 in debt. After being screwed over one time too many times, we sold our home in Texas and returned to California in June of 2006. Shortly after returning, Mike's mom passed away suddenly in December 2006. The suffering and struggling just didn't stop and a month after that, in January of 2007, I became pregnant and miscarried at three months. It was certainly a troubling time for us. A few weeks after that, Mike's Dad moved in with us. Then my other Grandma died. A couple of months later, the house we were renting went

ꕥ Restoring Your Beautiful Life

into foreclosure, and we had to move. Really, it was a blessing in disguise because it allowed us to break off on our own again while Mike's Dad went to live with friends.

We filed for bankruptcy in May of 2008, which was an extremely hard decision for me personally, but in the end, I am so grateful that we did. Mike and I were already miserable and the "D" word (divorce) was already being spoken. And then, the day that absolutely changed my life forever was July 4, 2008, when my dad died unexpectedly while taking a nap. It affected me more than I could have imagined!

I know that you hear people say it all the time, but, it's true. A part of me truly did die the day that my Dad passed. I didn't realize what an influence this man had in my life until he was gone. I was a Daddy's Girl, and I didn't even know it. I so wish that I would have taken the time to get to know him better. My Dad was my Dad, and I accepted him just as that. Sadly, I don't even know how he would have voted in the last Presidential elections.

My life has definitely changed since my Dad passed. Some of it for the worse and some of it for the better. But, in some strange way, like my Mom says, my Dad had to die in order for us (my Mom, my Brother and myself) to grow, and I truly believe that. There has been a lot of personal growth and changes for all of us since he died. Sadly, it took my Dad's passing to shape me more as the person I've always hoped and wanted to be.

Shortly before my Dad passed, I had just ordered the *You Can Heal Your Life* DVD by Louise L. Hay. It was delivered to my home the night before my Dad passed, and I didn't have a chance to watch it until a few months later. I was at a turning point in my life. I had recently lost my Dad, just quit a job that I hated, we had moved in with my Mom so that she wouldn't be living alone, and I was stuck in an unhappy and loveless marriage. There had to be more to life, right? I needed some hope in my life. I watched the movie, and it absolutely clicked with me. So, right away I ran out and bought the *You Can Heal Your Life* book by Louise L. Hay.

I read the book from cover to cover within hours, and I was hooked! I just had a sense of knowing that this could work for me. And it did! I was able to manifest things that I wanted very quickly – a job, money, an affordable place to rent.

It was incredible to think that my negative thoughts of today could really have an effect on all of my tomorrows. I began to look at my life in a totally different light. Not only could our thoughts change our life, but so could the pain and anger of events that we were still holding onto. These negative emotions could manifest themselves as disease or illness in my body.

About a year after I read the book and since my Dad had passed, Mike introduced me to an acquaintance of his named Scott. When this man came thru the door, I literally felt as though I had been hit by lightning. It was an incredibly powerful moment for me. It jolted me and made me realize that I couldn't go on living like this anymore. Not only was I cheating myself of true love, I was cheating Mike of love as well. More than anything, I wanted for Mike to have a chance at true, passionate love. This beautiful man deserved to know what real love was all about. I couldn't live this lie any longer but I was terrified of hurting Mike and breaking my daughter's heart by tearing apart her family. So, my marriage continued… but I began affirming for an amicable divorce.

From time to time, I would think about Scott but we didn't cross paths again for a few months. He started coming over to our house to visit with Mike often. During this time, I was reminded of a promise that Mike and I had made to one another shortly after getting married. We both agreed and promised that if either one of us ever reached the point of cheating, then it was time to end the marriage. I had reached that point. I was not only having thoughts about Scott, but I was beginning to take notice of other men. I would never cross the line and actually cheat on Mike, but my heart was screaming at me that it was time to get out of my marriage.

Mike and I decided in January 2010 that we were going to separate, and that he would move out on March 1st. It was important to us to give our daughter some time to get used to the idea. More important was that she could observe us being amicable with one another.

A few months after we did separate, Mike and I were playing the "Who is Your Type" game out of our friends, and I couldn't help but mention his friend, Scott. The next time Mike saw him; he gave him the green light to date me and encouraged him to ask me out for coffee. Scott and I slowly started becoming friends.

So, while Mike and I were separated, I began dipping my toes back into the dating pool and was having a lot of fun being the single girl. Scott and I continued to be friends and mainly texting buddies. During this time, I found out that he was still involved emotionally with a woman from his past. Knowing that, I kept my physical distance but mentally and emotionally, I was attracted to him.

I also just instinctively felt an incredible magnetic draw to him which I can't explain. I had never felt such an emotional bond to anyone else before. I was also caught up in the fantasy that the feeling of being struck by lightning when we first met had to mean something. There was rarely a day that would go by that we didn't chat via text. This man started to consume my thoughts, and I was fantasizing of a future together.

A couple of months passed and I ended up filing for divorce in July, 2010. It is important for me to state that I did not file for divorce because of my relationship with Scott. My marriage was over way before I ever laid eyes on Scott. After filing, I finally felt like I could breathe easy again. For the first time since Mike slipped the engagement ring on my finger, I can honestly say that I felt an incredible sense of inner peace…finally I was being true to myself.

Scott and I continued seeing each other casually during this time. All the while, I never let onto Mike that I was seeing Scott or that I had significant feelings for this man either. Even though Mike had given me his blessing to date Scott, I felt as though it would hurt Mike if he knew the truth.

I was fortunate enough to go to the Heal Your Life® training in September, 2010 to become a licensed Heal Your Life® teacher. It was an event that has changed my life forever. It has changed my thinking and given me a dream for where I want my career to go. I never had a dream before. Pretty sad, huh? It is also here where I finally started to break down my walls and barriers to both my head and heart.

I thought that I had it together emotionally, but what I really had was a tightly wound up ball of emotions and denial that I was afraid to express, admit or feel. It felt like the good, the bad and the ugly. It was here where the tears flowed, and the healing began. I never realized I had so much pent up inside of me. There is still so much remaining, I am continuing to peel back the layers of hurt, anger and rejection. It really is a process and one that I am so thankful that I am taking part in.

For several years, I was numb inside. It wasn't that I didn't feel emotions, I just couldn't relate to them. Everything felt dull. Does that make sense? A few months after my training, my heart started thawing out, and I was beginning to feel emotions again. They were painful and uncomfortable, yet at the same time, it was so wonderful to feel again. I felt like a little child feeling emotions for the first time! Then I started acting like a little child expressing those emotions, too. I found myself getting into little tiffs with Scott whereas normally, I would just suck it up if he said something that bothered me.

Scott and I would text every day, but rarely would I ever see him. He liked to keep me on the back burner but within arm's reach. Basically, I had become a booty call. When I was numb, I was willing to accept this type of relationship. But I was no longer numb, and this wasn't working for me anymore.

It was time to get honest with myself about my fantasy relationship with Scott. I started telling myself 'I am now living in the truth of the moment.' After affirming that for about a week, I knew what had to be done. So, I sent him an email telling him that this relationship worked when I was numb, and that if he wanted to continue to see me, then we needed to step it up and see if we had what it took to have a real relationship. We eventually talked on the phone, and he told me that he just wanted to be friends (no surprise there!), and that he didn't want for me to think that he had used me. I told him that that was fine. He then asked if I wanted to talk about it, and I said no. It was already humiliating enough to have the man of my dreams reject me, and there was no way in hell that I was going to let this man hear me crying over him.

When we stopped being texting buddies, I was truly broken-hearted without him. I can honestly say that I had never felt so empty inside like this before. For the first week, I felt like I could barely breathe. I was that pathetic woman who didn't want to get out of bed or even eat. My poor daughter didn't understand what was wrong with me; she just knew that Mommy was a complete wreck.

Even though we rarely saw one another, Scott had become a best friend of sorts and someone that I felt that I could reach out to at any time day or night. I had never experienced this type of deep bonding with anyone before. And I had never felt so shattered inside either, not even when Mike and I separated.

Mike, of course, noticed the difference in me, but I didn't dare tell him the truth. I told him that I had just broken it off with some guy, and he understood. Meanwhile, I was so upset that I ended up losing some weight without even trying - now that's a first for me!

While I was mourning the loss of my friendship with Scott, I realized that I was finally letting myself mourn the loss of my Dad and the loss of my marriage as well. Even though every waking moment literally was filled with emotional pain, and my heart had never felt so empty before, I began to feel an unbelievable amount of peace within. I had been holding onto so much hurt, pain, anger and resentment for many, many years, it was a relief to let some of the pain out and to let some of it go completely.

During this two-week period of mourning, I also apologized to my younger 25-year-old self. I felt that I had let myself down by marrying a man that I did not truly love. I was angry and sad that I had denied myself a possible life and marriage that could have been filled with passion and love. This was an incredible moment of self- forgiveness.

When I did that, I realized that had Mike not come into my life and blessed me with his love, I may have never truly known what healthy love could and should be like. You see, even though I may not have been in passionate love with this man, he showed me what a true, loyal, healthy and loving marriage should be. Mike set the bar high. He taught me to have standards for myself, something that I did not have before meeting him and something that I had forgotten in my obsession over Scott.

Two and half weeks after Scott and I had stopped talking and texting, he sent me a random text asking me how I was doing. I replied in a nice but curt manner. A couple of days later, he texted me again , and I was slowly starting to warm up to him. Eventually, he texted me and told me that he was seeing another woman that I knew and that is also a close friend of Mike's. He was all happy and bubbly, but honestly, it felt like he was trying to rub it in my face.

Ultimately, Scott and I ended up getting into an incredible fight, and he showed me a side of himself that I didn't know he possessed. He called me unforgivable names. He broke what was left of my heart. It was bad enough that he chose another woman over me but to then verbally attack me, that was stepping over the line. Not only did he step over the line, he then involved Mike by asking him questions and bringing him into our argument. The morning after this argument, I had to come clean with Mike and tell him my secret that I had been having a sexual relationship with this man.

It was at that moment of having to tell Mike the sordid truth that I was given the most incredible gift: Unconditional love.

> 66 Unconditional Love is holding love as a journey –
>
> not looking for a certain situation or outcome to fill an agenda
>
> and then taking it away when it doesn't happen
>
> the way you thought it should
>
> It's loving for the sake of loving because being love is who you are. 99
>
> *~ Talesha Hogan*

Mike forgave me right then and there. He told me that I hadn't betrayed him in any way. He told me that he had given us both the green light to date one another. He told me that even though the dynamics of our relationship had changed that he would still always be my best friend, that I could always count on him, and that he would always have my back. Can I just tell you how incredibly grateful and blessed I am to have this man in my life?!

Shortly before we separated in March, Mike started making phenomenal changes in his attitude and outlook on life. Without those changes, I don't know that we could be as amicable as we are today. Honestly and truly, our friends are amazed by the friendship and mutual respect that we share with one another.

Mike has told me that if it wasn't for my positive attitude and outlook on life, he doesn't know that he would have become the positive man that he is today. Awww…honestly, if it wasn't for him and his loving support throughout our marriage, I don't that I would have become the person that I am today. My life experience with him has shaped me into the person I am now, and for that I will forever be grateful.

It was incredibly important to me that we be able to show our daughter what a loving and amicable divorce could be like, and I am so proud to be able to say that we have done it and continue to do so. I feel that when it comes to divorce, both partners need to remember the love and respect that they felt for one another on their wedding day and carry that over into their divorce – not only for the sake of the children but for their sake as well.

66 Example is not the main thing in influencing others. 99

It is the only thing.

~ *Albert Schweitzer*

With my Heal Your Life® training and the support of my family and friends, I am beginning to explore what it means to feel again. Unearthing these old hurts is not a joyful experience, but being a healthier and happier person makes me feel sparkly inside.

This past year has taught me so much about myself. A very wise woman recently told me: *"What you are willing to put up with in your life is a clear indication of how mentally unhealthy you are."* Wow! I allowed myself to fall for a man who clearly didn't care about me. He would toss me some crumbs, and you would have thought that he had just handed me the moon. I AM loveable, worthy and deserving of a healthy, loving, passionate relationship filled with mutual respect, and I will now only accept the very BEST for myself.

I remember going to a fortune teller at a Renaissance Faire when I was in my early 20's. The woman told me that until I worked on myself, I would never really know true love. I recall leaving the faire that day feeling very agitated and angry with this woman for reasons that I couldn't quite explain.

As I look back now, I can now understand why I was upset with her, and why I left there that day feeling the way I did. When she told me that I had work to do on myself before I could ever really experience real love, what my sub-conscious mind heard was that who I was at that moment wasn't loveable, good enough, worthy or pretty enough to be loved. And sadly, not only did my subconscious mind hear that, it bought into it too. But, I was already emotionally unhealthy and had been feeling that way about myself for most of my life before I had ever crossed paths with the fortune teller. She just brought those emotions back up to surface.

The fortune teller was right. I have a lot of healing to do on myself before I can be a good partner to anyone or have the life that I desire. I was never taught how to love myself as a child or young adult. My parents didn't know how to do it for themselves, so of course they didn't know how to teach me how to do it for myself.

Because I didn't love myself, I never felt pretty or loveable and didn't feel deserving or worthy of attracting the man of my dreams or of having a good paying career. I have always felt *less than*. Up until recently, I had never even had a dream of what I wanted for myself and for my career. That is all changing. Through learning how to love myself, I now see that I AM SOMEBODY and I AM deserving and worthy of having a fabulous life filled with all the love, joy and happiness that I desire.

The past seven years have been filled with much struggle and grief, but I am at a point where I can look back and see how those struggles have made me stronger as a woman, wife, mother, daughter, sister, aunt and friend. Because of those experiences, I have been pushed onto a spiritual path that I may never have discovered if I hadn't been hurt and in pain and desperate for hope and peace within. I am extremely grateful for the path that I am now on. I still stumble from time to time but now I know that whether I succeed or not is my own doing. I am the master of my destiny and I now accept responsibility for myself.

66 Not until we are lost do we begin to understand ourselves. **99**

~ Henry David Thoreau

For so many years, I was angry and bitter at Mike because in my head, I felt he was to blame for me marrying him and ultimately denying myself passion and love with someone else. Clearly, I don't feel that way anymore. I now am able to accept responsibility for my actions. I had a choice, and I chose to marry him – nobody forced me. Now that I have acknowledged that and really understand that, I am free to let it go and move on with my life. By letting it go, I have been able to let so many more positive opportunities and relationships into my life. We unknowingly hold our anger like a shield of protection and push people and opportunities away. It's time to put down the shield and welcome love and joy back into my heart.

66 Each of us has the right and the responsibility

to assess the road which lies ahead

and those over which we have traveled,

and if the feature road looms ominous or unpromising,

and the road back uninviting – inviting,

then we need to gather our resolve

and carrying only the necessary baggage,

step off that road into another direction.

If the new choice is also unpalatable, without embarrassment,

we must be ready to change that one as well. **99**

~ Maya Angelou

There was a time in my life when I looked at my decision to marry Mike as a fork in the road and felt that I had chosen the wrong path. I know now that isn't true. Marrying Mike was my spoon in the road. The journey that I shared with this man, and the love and support that he has given me along the way has brought me to my most authentic self, a place inside of myself that I may have never discovered if we didn't cross paths.

I believe we all experience those "spoons in our roads" to assist us on our journey for the life we were created to live.

JODY KRATZ
Chapter 7 & 8:

Change Starts From Within
& Creating My Beautiful Life

CHAPTER 7
Change Starts From Within

❝ Time for a Change

My spirit is nudging me

Saying it's time for a change

It is time for me to see

Where I am and rearrange

I hear my intuition

I can no longer ignore

I can bring to fruition

The life I dream and long for **❞**

~ Jody Kratz

Major life changes must start from within. Your outer world cannot change until you change your inner world. You have to take a long, hard look at your life, and how it has been working for you. This is not an easy task but a necessary one. We come into this world a blank slate, and the well meaning people around us start from day one to fill our mind with their thoughts and beliefs about how the world should be perceived.

What were the beliefs you were taught? Were they limiting, negative beliefs, or were they positive? We all probably received a little of both depending on the subject. These beliefs from early on are still affecting your life today. Make a list of the beliefs and behavior patterns in every area of your life. Which thoughts and behaviors serve you? Which do not? Do you have behaviors that you picked up from watching how your parents handled situations?

Really look at your life and see which beliefs and behavior patterns are negatively affecting the quality of your life. This is the first step in creating change. Your outer world is a reflection of your inner world. If you are not happy with your life, you have to change yourself. You are responsible for your happiness, nothing outside of you is to blame. You cannot change those things that you are not aware of, so start your journey of self discovery now.

66 If you don't like something, change it.

If you can't change it, change your attitude. **99**

~ Maya Angelou

Many of us women were raised to believe that we had to take care of everyone's wants and needs but our own. We witnessed our mothers just give and give and never ask for anything in return. Where did it get them? Do they have regrets now that their children are grown and life has passed them by? Let me tell you a little about my life and the negative thoughts and behavior patterns I discovered.

My real name is Joanne but I have been called Jody my whole life. I was born in 1960 and grew up in the suburbs of Philadelphia. I am the youngest of four children, but really more of an only child. Philip was 8 years older, Chip 10 years, and Susan 12 years older. Chip and Susan were off to college and out of the house by the time I was 8.

My father owned a home heating oil business and was rarely home. He would get called in the middle of the night and have to go out on service calls. My mother ran the business from home, and the phone rang all day long.

Money was never an issue growing up, and I always had everything I wanted. It wasn't used as a reward or taken away as punishment, it was just always there. That has been a big help throughout my life. I don't have negative beliefs about money. I view it as a positive energy; it comes to me; I give it away and even more comes back to me in return. I can't say the same about other areas of my life.

Chip and Susan always seemed to me like they were raised in a different family. They went off to college and lived happily ever after. I'm sure they have had their ups and downs but they have led relatively normal and happy lives. Then my brother, Philip, and I came. My mother always says she doesn't know what happened when it came to the two of us.

She loved us very much, and we were raised the same as Chip and Susan, but we seemed to be the problem children. Many decades later, and after much soul searching I think I know the reason why. My father suffered from depression and was a functioning alcoholic. He never missed a day of work. Philip inherited the depression gene and had drug and alcohol problems. Chip and Susan were out of the house before Philip's issues were full blown, and my father's issues became worse. I was raised in a very different environment than Chip and Susan. Thank God, I didn't inherit that depression gene, or I probably wouldn't be alive to write this.

I was taught to step on eggshells and don't rock the boat. That's how it is when you live with depressed people that have substance abuse problems. I was taught to be an enabler from day one. I'm still not sure if it's worse to be the enabler or the depressed drunk. At least the drunk doesn't remember what he put the enabler through. Lord knows the enabler would never rub the abusers' nose in their poor behavior, not that it would do any good anyway.

It was all swept under the rug, never to be spoken of again. Incident after incident was ignored, and we pretended everything was normal until the next time. It was like living the movie Groundhog Day. This theme repeated itself my entire life, and I didn't even realize the connection until I started on my spiritual path in my late thirties.

My earliest childhood memories are of my father coming home late at night from work drunk. He would say hello, and my mother would heat up his dinner, and he would go to bed. He was never mean or abusive from what I remember. He was annoying when he was drunk and would repeat himself over and over.

I can remember as a teenager hanging out at Steele Field with a bunch of friends, and a car was coming down the road weaving side to side. My big mouth yelled laughingly, "look at that idiot." My friend turned to me and said, "Jody, that's your dad." I hopped in my car and went home to make sure he got there safely. It was embarrassing but not the first or last time his drinking would humiliate me in front of my friends.

I can remember on weekends he would always sneak into the kitchen to the liquor cabinet, and we could hear the bottles rattling as he snuck a shot. My mother never said anything to him, and as the day progressed, he would become more intoxicated. He would go in the kitchen and we would shake our heads and roll our eyes, but nobody ever said anything. Summer was my father's slow season, and we would go on vacation. He was a different person on vacation. He was relaxed, and we had a lot of fun. We would go to my grand mom and grand pop's house in Wildwood, New Jersey. They were my father's parents.

My father would take us to the beach, and we would play in the sand together. We would find clams, and he would open them and feed the seagulls. He loved to swim in the ocean. Then we would go to visit my mother's parents in Miami, Florida. We would go see all of the attractions, and it felt like we were a normal family. Every summer we went both places until I was in my teens.

After I was married and had children of my own, I asked my mother why she stayed with him. She said that at the time it would have been almost impossible to leave him and support four children. Women did not have the options in the early sixties that are available to them today. She stayed so we would have a nice home and be able to go to college.

She also told me about my father's depression. I had never known. She said he was always threatening to commit suicide, and some days it was all she could do to encourage him to get up and go to work for another day. After I was born, the gynecologist told my mother to let him kill himself if that's what he wants; it's not something you have control over.

So for all of those years she propped him up and kept him going. She managed to do this and keep it a secret. That is where I learned that you are supposed to sacrifice everything for the family. You don't speak up, and you pretend everything is normal. She told me that you have to let the man think he is the boss and be supportive when really you are the one in charge. I was taught how to manipulate men into thinking they were making all of the decisions when really it was me.

My mother was always steady like a rock; she still is my rock today. She is now 84 years old and the only consistent source of love and support I have ever had. She has so much wisdom from her years of misery. She always listens patiently to my rants and says: "This, too, shall pass." She has always made me believe that I could be whatever I wanted to be.

Even now as I am laid off from my job, she encourages me to follow my dreams. I know that she is concerned and wishes I would go and get a "real job," but she is still supportive of me and doesn't question or criticize. She has always had a knack for keeping the peace and keeping up appearances except where Philip was concerned.

Philip was eight years older than me, and I adored him. I never knew the entire story about my father while growing up but my mother couldn't always hide what was going on with Philip. My mother told me she knew Philip was different even as a baby. She said he was very sensitive and would cry when he heard sad music. He didn't do well in school like Chip and Susan had. Once he became a teenager, he developed drug and alcohol problems.

My first knowledge of his drug use was when I was about 14 years old. He made me go into the bathroom with him and locked the door. I can still picture it vividly in my mind. The tub on the left, the sink and the toilet on the right, a window looking over the back yard straight ahead, and peach colored towels on the rack.

Restoring Your Beautiful Life

Philip proceeded to take out a baggie with white powder. It was methamphetamine. He melted it with water on a spoon and drew it up in a syringe. He took off his black braided leather belt with a big silver buckle and tightened it around his upper arm. He stuck the needle in his arm, drew back blood then plunged the drug into his vein.

I was dizzy and sick to my stomach. He said to me, "This is to teach you a lesson; if I ever catch you doing drugs, I will kill you." It worked, I never really did get into drugs, I smoked pot but after all it was the seventies. My girlfriends and I just loved him. He and his friends seemed to be so cool and fun. He told me when I was fifteen that I was only allowed to drink alcohol with him. He would bring me to a bar that the family of one of his friends owned. We would have so much fun listening to music and hanging out with his friends. He would buy alcohol for me and my friends as long as we drank at home and didn't go out.

I once had a science project due, and he stayed up all night making paper machete planets and spray painting them florescent colors. I didn't realize it was the methamphetamine. He was very outgoing and fun, everyone liked him. No one saw the dark side except my mother.

There were nights when she would stay up with him all night talking to him. I could hear him sobbing. The older he got, the worse it became. My mother sent him to a psychiatrist but he admitted to my mother he didn't tell him the truth because he was afraid the psychiatrist wouldn't like him if he knew the truth. His girlfriend that he loved very much broke up with him, and things really got out of control. He ended up being committed to a mental institution. I went to visit him once, and it was so traumatic for me that my mother didn't bring me again.

It was like a scene out of a movie. There were people yelling and cursing, a girl sitting curled up in the corner rocking back and forth crying. There was another person watching TV in a straight jacket. There was no way my beloved brother belonged there.

The highlight of the visit was when a girl had jujubee's, which were a popular candy back then. She had a mouthful and dropped a few on the floor. I don't know what happened, but attendants came from everywhere and tackled the poor girl on the floor. People were yelling that they were only candy, but they thought that she had a mouthful of pills. It turned into a brawl with patients and hospital employees, it was mass confusion. I was never so glad to leave a place in my life.

My mother claims he was misdiagnosed as bi-polar. She thought he just had depression. Looking back now, as a Registered Nurse, I would have to agree with my mother. The psychiatrist probably saw him high on methamphetamine and assumed he was manic because my brother didn't tell him the truth about the drugs. He was put on Lithium and Thorazine which didn't help. He stopped taking the medication because he said he didn't want to depend on drugs the rest of his life to feel normal. But he didn't seem to have a problem continuing the illegal drugs and alcohol. I have always been intuitive for as long as I can remember. I didn't think anything of it, I thought that was the way everyone experienced things. I also had a strong inner voice that I didn't realize was my spirit guiding me, and I unfortunately learned to tune it out most of my adult life.

One warm summer night in 1977, I was 17 years old and had my friend, Terri, stay overnight at my house. My friend, Dan, came over to visit and hang out for a while. After Dan left, Philip and I got into an argument because he really liked Dan and felt that I just used him when I didn't have anything better to do. We had a heated exchange of words, and then he went out with his friends. Terri and I eventually fell asleep.

I woke up very early in the morning hysterical, then woke Terri up and said, "Something is wrong, I think Philip is dead." She said, "You must have had a nightmare go back to sleep." I heard my parents downstairs, which wasn't unusual, they were early risers.

I don't know why, but I went to the window and looked out into the backyard and there was a body by the swimming pool covered in a gold sheet. I ran downstairs, and my father was just sitting with his head in his hands sobbing. I had never seen my father cry before. I wanted to go outside but they wouldn't let me. Philip had shot himself in the head at the age of 25. My mother said he wouldn't have done it if he was sober. The police came, and the rest of the day was pretty much a blur.

I don't really remember much about the funeral except that I had never seen so many people at a funeral. My mother said she had never seen such a long procession of cars and that my brother would be happy with that. After the funeral, everyone came back to our house.

My sister, Susan, was there running the show. She was angry that everyone was drinking and hanging around. But that is how Philip would have wanted it, so I told her to go fuck herself. My sister took everything of Philip's and got rid of it. I was so angry. I did manage to get one of his favorite shirts without her knowing about it. She said it was not good for me to hold on to things of his. I think my mother was too grief stricken to stop her. Looking back, I think my sister did that because we were raised not to talk about things and pretend everything was normal.

True to form, things went back to normal, and we didn't discuss it. I know it killed my mother inside but she just kept moving forward. She told me many years later after my father had passed away, that there was nothing worse than losing a child. She said "you can replace a man, but you can't replace a child."

She held so much in over the years. She is the strongest person emotionally that I know. She is very loving, but she doesn't believe in feeling sorry for yourself. No matter what, you keep moving forward. That is one lesson that has served me well. She always taught personal responsibility. If I did something wrong and tried to blame someone else she would say, "If they jumped off a bridge would you follow?" She always held me accountable for my own actions which also served me well.

My brother's death had a profound effect on me. I don't suffer from depression but can remember threatening to kill myself once or twice to a boyfriend just for attention. I must admit I was a drama queen as a teenager.

One night I was driving home very drunk and driving way too fast approaching a curve. I saw someone standing in the middle of the road and had to slam on my breaks. It was my dead brother, Philip. I could see him clear as day, and when I came to a stop he just faded away. He had saved my life. It was very eerie, but I felt the love and knew he was watching over me.

I drank heavily until I was 20 years old. I put my mother through a few years of hell. I wouldn't come home at night or even bother to call. I suffered anxiety attacks for a few years after my brother died. My heart would race, I felt like my throat was closing and I couldn't breathe. I would have to lie down. When it would happen in public, it was like an out of body experience. Everything would close in around me, and I felt like I wasn't in my body. It was so frightening that I hated going anywhere alone.

I went to the doctor and told him about the attacks, and that my throat would close and I couldn't swallow or breathe. He said it was allergies and gave me an antihistamine to take when the symptoms occurred. It was anxiety! The attacks went away in a few years when I came to terms with my brother's death.

There were rumors that my brother didn't commit suicide, that he was murdered over drugs. Of course, I latched right onto that notion, rather than think he would do that to all of us. I had so much guilt that we had an argument the night he died. I finally realized in my late twenties that he did indeed shoot himself in the head.

There was another life-altering event that also contributed to my drinking and wild behavior. In April of 1976, I had an abortion. I had just turned 16 in March, and he was 17. He was the first boy I had ever been with, and I, of course, thought we were in love. He talked me into having an abortion, and not long after that he had a new girlfriend. I hated him for a long time, but forgave him decades before I forgave myself. The guilt over having the abortion was horrendous.

Teenagers always talk, and everyone found out. There was one guy who called me a murderer. Many of my friends had abortions, and I had no idea what they had gone through. My little inner voice had once again told me don't do it and once again I ignored it. The guilt ate away at me until I was in my 40's and finally forgave myself. I was always afraid if I ever had children that something horrible would happen to them because I had an abortion and didn't deserve to be a mother.

I don't know why I didn't tell my mother. She would have understood and been supportive like she always was. I think I didn't tell her because of what she was going through with Philip. It was the year before he died. Back then, you didn't need parental consent for an abortion, they didn't give you counseling, you paid the $130, and that was it.

My mother eventually found out a few months later when she overheard me crying about it on the phone. She wasn't angry and didn't judge me. She said I should have come to her. Over the next few months I kept getting sick. I was hospitalized once, and they said I had colitis. The guilt was literally making me ill. The symptoms kept getting worse, and in November I ended up in the hospital for 10 days.

I had an exploratory surgery by a gynecologist because of the location of the pain. Then they had to call in the general surgeon because my appendix had ruptured, and I had peritonitis. The infection was so severe I almost died. It's a known fact that extreme feelings such as hate, anger, and guilt can cause disease. The guilt over the abortion was killing me.

> **❝** Guilt is the source of sorrow, 'this the fiend, Th' avenging fiend,
>
> That follows us behind, With whips and sings. **❞**
>
> ~ *Nicholas Rowe*

I graduated from high school in 1978 and started at Penn State in the fall. I had a positive PPD but no signs of TB, so the doctor thought perhaps it was in the abdominal cavity, given all the problems I had in the past with the peritonitis. (A PPD is a test for Purified Protein Derivative and is a diagnostic tool for tuberculosis.)

The doctor said I would never have children. I was devastated and knew it was punishment for having an abortion. I attended the local campus of Penn State because I had a boyfriend and didn't want to leave home. I had a part-time job at a clothing store. I had a 4.0 average and was doing well but I was still drinking a lot on the weekends.

My boyfriend who happened to be bi-polar (start of sick men pattern) broke up with me in February. I was so upset I dropped out of school to be the assistant manager at the clothing store. I thought that was a good opportunity at the time. I started drinking more again.

My mother was at her wits end that I was 19 and going nowhere with my life. She took me somewhere to do testing, that cost a fortune, to find out what occupation I would be best suited for. They told her I had an above average IQ and could be anything I wanted to be, but the psychological tests showed that all I wanted to be was a mother. I guess that went back to the guilt about the abortion, and it just rubbed in the fact that I was told I would never have children.

My mother and I still laugh today that she spent all that money to find out I could be anything I wanted to be, just to find out all I wanted was to be a mother.

I met my future husband, Bill, around the time I turned twenty. My friend, Grace, wanted to go see this guy, Jimmy, because she was going to be moving to Arizona. I told her I didn't feel like going with her, and I wanted to go home. Because she was moving, she used manipulation and made me feel guilty, so I gave in. All the while, my inner voice was saying: DON'T GO. We went and met Jimmy and his friends.

We were drinking beer and having a great time. Everybody was ready to go home at around one in the morning, but there was still beer left! Bill suggested that we hang out and drink the beer. It was love at first sight; he was so much fun and charming. We ended up going to Wildwood, New Jersey for a few days.

It was the most incredible time of my life. We thought we were soul mates, and he carried scars on both of his wrists for the rest of his life from the old fashioned bed spread with the little raised bumps on the bed in the hotel. Needless to say, it was quite a magical time. I just loved him and kept thinking how much he reminded me of my brother, Philip. At the time, I didn't make the connection.

When we went back home to reality, my mother was furious. I had a boyfriend at the time, and I was not a cheater, so I told him what had happened. He was a really nice, normal guy, and he wanted to work things out. I thought about it, then decided he was right that Bill was too wild. But, I couldn't get Bill out of my mind, and he kept calling. My inner voice told me not to do it, and again, I ignored it. Bill and I had a few months of fun and partying. We were back in Wildwood in August, bar hopping and having a ball. While we were walking down the street, I suddenly started vomiting. I couldn't figure out what the problem was. It turns out I was pregnant. I couldn't believe it! After I was told I would never have children.

I quit drinking but was still in denial about the situation. My mother came to me when I was about three months along and asked me if I was pregnant. She said she knew because I hadn't had a period in a few months. I had never considered what I was going to do about it. Bill and I wanted the baby but hadn't made any plans or told our parents yet. I was 20, and he was 23 and owned a house.

My mother said if you are going to keep the baby, then you should move in with him now and get to know each other better before the baby is born. She was always very wise. We had only known each other a few months before I became pregnant. I moved in with him to begin our new life. The house was a row house (they call them townhomes now) in a lower middle class neighborhood. We didn't have a yard, we had a back alley. I had grown up in an upper middle class neighborhood with a pool and a large back yard. I cried for three days straight after I moved in because I missed my home and my parents. Poor Bill must have been wondering what he had gotten himself into.

I finally adjusted, and we were so happy about having the baby. His parents were embarrassed because we weren't married but they were excited about the baby. I didn't like his mother, Mildred, at first; she would just say whatever popped into her head without thinking. She had always controlled Bill by either screaming or crying and carrying on.

He had a brief marriage when he was very young because she didn't like them living together. He had cancelled the wedding four times, but eventually they got married at a justice of the peace. The first time our parents met, she told them, "You would love Bill's first wife, Chrissy. She is such a nice girl." I couldn't believe it! My parents just looked at each other, and Bill's father, Herb, just looked embarrassed.

I refused to walk down the aisle pregnant so we planned to get married after the baby was born. I was Presbyterian, and Bill was Catholic. Bill's mother was a Catholic convert and very adamant that the baby had to be Catholic or he would go to hell. She was serious! I told her I wasn't converting when Bill didn't even go to mass. She was crying and carrying on so Bill started going to mass again.

William G. Kratz, Jr. was born May 5th, 1982, not long after my 21st birthday. He was the first grandchild on both sides of the family, and we had a lot of support. Yes, he was christened Catholic, and Mildred was pleased. She had gotten her way once again.

Bill and I were very happy together, and things were going well. When I went for my six-week check up after Billy was born and told the doctor I hadn't had a period yet, she said I was pregnant. Jimmy was born on March 25th, 1983. Billy was 10 months old. Thank God, I had Mildred and my mom.

The young priest in our parish would not christen Jimmy or marry us because he said we should have gotten married after Billy was born. I was outraged and asked him how he could refuse to christen an innocent baby. I told Mildred that my children and I would never step foot in a Catholic church again. She cried and carried on and got the elderly Monsignor of her parish to christen Jimmy and marry Bill and me on August 25th, 1983. I never could figure out why the young priest was so draconian and the elderly priest was so kind. But then, Mildred did give a whole lot of money to her parish and volunteered at the church. I guess that's a rather cynical view of the situation.

A few months after we were married I was pregnant yet again. I guess you have to take the diaphragm out of the bedside drawer in order for it to be effective. Bill was very overwhelmed by the third pregnancy. Michael was born October 25th, 1984. Billy was only two and Jimmy was 18 months old. Thank God for grandparents. I had three babies in diapers.

While I was in the hospital after I had Michael, my mom and Bill bought a single home in Havertown where we had grown up. I didn't even see the house, but it was such a great price they had to buy it while they could. I should say my mother bought the house. She and my father paid cash for the house, and we would pay them back. She didn't want her grandchildren to grow up in a row house without a yard. That is how my mother is; she wants the best for her family.

I was attracted to my husband because he reminded me of Philip; he was fun, and spontaneous. Those qualities that I loved in him turned into qualities that drove me crazy. My inner voice kept saying "Oh, this isn't good." There were so many red flags, but I ignored all of them because I loved him so much.

Since the day we met, he had told me he would be dead by the age of 40. He didn't know why, but he said he couldn't picture himself being alive past 40. He was the type that would go out for milk and not come home until six hours later. He would say, I stopped at the bar and everybody would buy me drinks. He drank every night but only got really drunk occasionally. He went through several jobs and always ended up quitting. It was never his fault, there was always someone treating him unfairly. I believed and defended him, but in the back of my mind I was starting to wonder.

Somewhere along the line I went from being his best friend and lover to being his mother. I was taking care of him and telling him what to do and how to do it. It was not a partnership. My mother kept telling me I needed to get an education so that I would be able to support myself and the kids if necessary. She didn't want to see me end up like her; stuck in an unhappy marriage and unable to leave because of money. But every time I went back to school, I ended up being pregnant again. When I was 24 years old, I finally had my tubes tied after Michael was born.

Bill's drinking continued to get worse. My father owned a home heating business and sent Bill to truck driving school and then hired him to drive an oil transport tractor trailer. He did well with that for a while but became bored. He had an opportunity to buy a landscaping business, and my parents gave us the money to buy the business. It worked out well because my father wanted to sell his business and retire, so he helped Bill with the business.

I was attending community college to get an associate's degree in medical administrative assistant. I decided we would need benefits, so I took a job at a local hospital working every weekend and every holiday in the

Emergency Department registration. I was the one who asked for insurance information while people were in agony.

Bill was drinking heavily but was great with the kids. He took them all kinds of places on the weekends. He even would take them to the beach for the weekend. Three boys that close in age would have been a handful for anyone by themselves, but he did it and really loved it.

I was one class away from my associate's degree when my little inner voice said you should be a nurse. THIS time I didn't ignore it. I switched my major, then pretty much had to start over. I did an 18-month program and had my associate's degree in nursing in December of 1991 at 31 years old.

Bill's drinking had continued to worsen; while I was in nursing school he started to say he wished he was dead. I would talk to him for hours and try to build him up. I was doing exactly what my mother did with Philip.

He always was saying if I had " this," then I would be happy. The thing he wanted always changed but nothing ever made him happy. He decided that we should move away from Havertown and start a new life then he would be happy. He said he would be able to quit drinking because he wouldn't be around the old crowd.

I told him you can't run away from your problems, they just follow you. My little voice said that moving was a mistake and wouldn't solve anything. I ignored my inner voice yet again because I loved him so much, I would do anything to make him happy. My parents helped us buy a house in Downingtown, and we moved in August of 1991 before I graduated from nursing school.

When my father passed away, Bill's downward spiral began. He adored my father and said he felt like he was the father he never had. Everything had always been about Bill, never about me. He was never there for me. He was so upset when my father died, he was unable to go to the gathering after the funeral. I had to go alone with the kids.

I now lived an hour away from my family, friends, and work. As a new nurse, they would make you work full time for one year until you were experienced. Bill really started to deteriorate. It was no surprise that moving did not make him happy, it made him worse. I was working full time, eight-hour shifts, and they had me doing all three of the possible shifts in one week. For example, I would be on day shift for a day or two, then evening shift, then night shift by the end of the week. I couldn't adjust and was getting sick a lot. Bill told me that I couldn't handle the shift changes, and that I should get on a steady shift. The only steady shift available was 3 p.m. to 11:30 p.m.

Eventually, I did four eight-hour shifts and four twelve-hour shifts in a two-week period, which gave me three days a week off. Because I worked an hour away, by the time I got home and fell asleep it would be about 2:30 a.m. I would get up at 6 a.m. and make breakfast for the kids and get them off to school. Bill still had his landscaping business, but all of his customers were now an hour away. Within a year, my mother bought a home in Downingtown so she could help me.

Bill's spontaneity that I loved so much when we were young, now angered me to no end. He went to work when he felt like it, and if something more interesting came up, he didn't go to work. One day, I watched him load his truck with all of his equipment and leave for work. Thirty minutes later, he was back at home, so I assumed he had forgotten something. He said, "I just saw the truck stocking the creek with trout! I've got to go fishing!" Another day of work pushed off to a future day. I had to call all of the customers and make an excuse.

Not only did I work full time, but I ran his business and did all of the paperwork and billing. I also had to clean the house and do the wash and check the homework. I was becoming filled with resentment.

His depression continued to get worse, and he talked about death a lot. He decided he would be happy if he had a motorcycle. He thought it would be so great to have that feeling of freedom. So he got a motorcycle and was happy for about a month.

I was working on the surgical cardiac step-down unit as an RN, but I always wanted to work in the Emergency Department. In 1994, they had an opening in the ED. The problem was that it was evening shift, five days a week. My inner voice said: "You need a day job to be home with your family." Once again, I didn't listen. You think I would have learned by now. But the only day jobs available were in nursing homes, and I didn't want to work in a nursing home.

I told myself that I would take the job in the ED, and when a spot opened there on day shift, I would switch. I regretted that decision for many years and had a lot of guilt. I felt that I should have taken any day job I could have gotten to be home to take care of my family. Hindsight is 20/20. Add that to the list of things I needed to forgive myself for.

We had a severe ice storm in January of 1994 and lost power for three days.

Bill was obsessed with staying home and trying to keep the baseboard heat pipes warm with little sterno cans. There was no electric, heat, water, or telephone. I took the kids to my mother's.

We thought everything was fine when the electric was restored, but it wasn't. When the heater started running, the ice in the pipes expanded, and all of the baseboard pipes exploded. There was water everywhere and no heat again. Homeowner's insurance covered the water damage but not the plumbing.

I don't know why he was so wild about it all. There was nothing that could change it, and we had it fixed. He had himself so worked up he had chest pain. He was 37 years old, and his biological father and all of his uncles had died in their early forties of heart disease. I took him to the closest hospital where he was admitted with dangerously high blood pressure. They ruled out a heart attack and sent him home the next day. They never did a CAT scan of his head even though his blood pressure was so high, and he had numbness on his left side. But they just put him on blood pressure medication. I have always believed he had a stroke because after that episode he became downright bizarre and was a totally different person.

I didn't have much confidence in psychiatrists after Philip, but I had to do something. I found a psychiatrist, and Bill agreed to go. Psychiatrists for some reason make agreements with patients and expect that they will do what they agreed upon or tell the truth about it. Bill was put on Xanax for anxiety and Paxil for depression under the condition he would not drink. Well, he didn't stop drinking, and he became really crazy and paranoid. He had always owned a gun but he started buying a whole collection of hand guns, rifles, and semiautomatics. He said that he was getting ready for the "uprising" and had to protect our family. When he was sober, he wasn't paranoid and would laugh about the things he had said.

In the spring of 1994, disaster struck again. Bill developed diverticulitis and had to have major abdominal surgery. He wouldn't be able to work for about three months and would have lost his landscaping business, so we sold it. After that, he really became obsessed with suicide. So many nights I would come home from work exhausted and have to talk to him. I would cry and beg him not to kill himself. The children loved their father so much, I never told them about the late night suicide threats.

Losing the business was the worst thing that could have happened to him. During this time, I got two strange phone calls from customers. These two women didn't know each other but claimed that Bill told them I made him live in the garage, and that he was going to leave me to be with them. Evidently, he had been having affairs with these women and then dumped them. He tried to deny it and say they were crazy. But how could two different women have the exact same story when they didn't know each other? How many more were there?

I was devastated. I never saw it coming, I loved him so much. I couldn't put him out, he had just had major surgery, he was suicidal, and the kids worshipped him. I had a million excuses. It wasn't the money because I was the one supporting us. My little voice kept telling me to get him out of the house! I ignored the voice again.

Bill got a part-time job at the mall at Christmas time which seemed to cause his attitude to improve. Little did I know he was having an affair with a woman named Sandy that he met at the bar. I found out when I got a phone call at work in early 1995 that Bill had been arrested for driving under the influence. He had the kids in the car, and he was going well over 50 in a 35 mile per hour zone. He lost control of the car and hit a sign that plowed almost into the front seat.

The police said it was a miracle that no one was killed. God was surely watching over them because the kids didn't have a scratch on them. I went to the police station, and Bill was so drunk. He was not in touch with reality at all. He told me he had special powers, and he could escape from the jail anytime he wanted. He thought he could fly. He said he was going to kill himself as soon as he got home.

The police told me because it was such a small station, they couldn't possibly keep him all night, and that I had to take him home. Luckily, I was an ED nurse and knew better. I told them to have him committed to a Psychiatric institution but they balked, because they didn't feel like going through all the legal paperwork. So out of desperation, I threatened to sue them and call the newspapers if anything happened to him or my family. Thus began Bill's first visit to the psychiatric ward.

I found out from the kids that they had been at daddy's friend, Sandy's, house. He was having an affair with a woman that would let him drive that drunk with his children. How dare he take them to her house while I'm out supporting the family?

He was only hospitalized for about a week, then they sent him for occupational counseling. They did all kinds of tests and said that he had brain damage they thought was from a fall from the attic as a child. I have no doubt the brain damage was from the undiagnosed stroke he had the year before. The psychiatrist said it was possible because certain strokes cause extreme changes in personality.

I never told anyone at work what went on at home. They would laugh when the kids would call and say they had cereal for dinner. They had no idea it was because their father was passed out drunk. Most of the time it was my mother who made sure they had dinner and the homework was done.

May of 1995, right before Billy's 13th birthday, Bill had a terrible episode of depression. I got a phone call at work about 10:30 p.m. It was Bill's brother, Bob, who said that Bill called him drunk and was threatening to kill himself. He wanted Bob to come watch a movie with him. Instead of going and helping his brother he called the police and told them that Bill had a houseful of guns. I had to leave work.

I was so angry with Bob for calling the police. Why couldn't he have just gone over and watched a movie and spent time with his brother? Bill had been so depressed since the DUI. He had no job, he felt the kids were getting older and didn't have time for him anymore. He didn't realize they were older, could see what was going on and were probably avoiding him. The hour ride home was torture. I was used to driving home and never quite knowing what I was going to walk into, but this was different with the police involved. I got home, and there were two police cars in front of the house. I asked them to leave, and they wouldn't go. I went in the house, and Bill was just happy to see me. He didn't even know the police were outside.

I went back out and explained that I was home, and everything was fine. They wanted me to go back in to see if he would come out and talk to them. Bill did not like the police, and he refused to go talk to them. I spent some time pleading with him, but it was no use. When I went back outside, there was a huge mobile command unit, police cars lined all the way up the street, and snipers in the woods. I was horrified.

They told me I was not allowed back in the house. I told them: "My children are in the house, and he has no idea you're out here. Let me go back in my house!" But they would not allow it. They had me in the mobile command center, and I had them call Bill's psychiatrist. The psychiatrist spoke with Bill and told the police that he was not an immediate danger to himself or others. They still wouldn't let me go in the house. They had their own crisis intervention person call and speak to Bill, and that person also said he was not an immediate danger to anyone.

But the police said they had seen tragedies like this before, and they weren't leaving. They told me to call Bill and have him send the kids out. I told them that was ridiculous, they were sleeping and had no idea what was going on but they insisted that I do it. Our street has no street lights or sidewalks, and it was pitch black.

Bill opened the door to let the kids out, and when I started to go get them, the police held me back. It took about six of them to hold me back – I was crying, kicking, punching, screaming, and trying to go get my babies. The police were furious and threatened to arrest me. So much for compassion. They said they wouldn't let me get them in the dark because my husband may have shot us all. I informed him that if he shot my children then I would rather be shot right along with them.

The police were horrible, and I was livid at the whole situation. I took the kids to my mother's house and spoke to Bill on the phone. He was drunk but in good spirits. He was having a ball messing with the police. He kept letting the dog out, who would immediately run to the hidden swat team. Bill would then poke his head out the door and laugh at them and call them names. There were helicopters; it was all over the news.

Bill finally passed out. He called me in the morning and asked, "Why are there police all over the neighborhood?" He didn't remember much from the night before. He didn't understand why they were doing this when nothing bad happened. I was scared to death that the police might try to shoot him through the windows. He told me to call them and say he was coming out.

I drove to the house and got there as he was coming out. He had his hands in the air and was very calm. Those bastards rushed him and attacked him. He suffered a broken ankle and cuts and bruises. That was not only unnecessary, but was certainly not the way to treat someone who was mentally ill.

The aftermath was a disaster for our family. It was all over the television news and in the newspapers. They said he had a standoff with police. In reality, he never showed a weapon and was passed out for most of the so called "standoff." I couldn't keep the kids home from school forever. I couldn't stay home from work forever either.

Most of the neighbors were kind and compassionate, but there were some that treated us like the scum of the earth. People have no idea the profound effect mental illness has on a family. Billy's birthday was ruined, but that was the least of our worries. Bill was kept in the psychiatric ward for a court-ordered 30 days.

ꝏ Restoring Your Beautiful Life

Although I was really upset and angry over what had happened, it was such a relief not to have him around the house. I didn't have to worry about what would happen next. This was not the person I married. I had no idea who he was anymore.

Things were even worse when he got out in 30 days. He was so ashamed and humiliated for what he had done to the family. The police had confiscated all of his guns after the incident and would not give them back, so he started buying replacements.

I called the police and asked how he could be allowed to buy guns? What was the point of confiscating the original ones? They said it was legal for him to buy guns because he was never charged with anything from the incident.

The next year was pure hell. There were nightly threats of suicide. I would beg, cry, and plead with him. One night I was particularly exhausted, and he had himself locked in the office with a gun saying he was going to shoot himself. I started the usual crying and pleading and the little voice inside said, "Stop, enough is enough."

I told Bill, "Don't you dare kill yourself in our house or on our property. My brother did that, and my poor father had to find him." I told him I was through begging and pleading, and if that is what he wanted to do, then go right ahead and do it. I was tired of being held hostage with these emotional games. I went upstairs and went to bed. He didn't kill himself. The next year was more of the same. My mother was going to Florida with her sister from January of 1996 until March. Bill said winter was very hard on him and made him so depressed. He felt if he could just go away for awhile, then he would be happy. My mother offered to rent Bill a trailer in Florida until March, if he would drive her and my aunt there. I know she only did this to get him out of my hair.

The boys and I went to visit him for a week in February, and he seemed almost like his old self. But when he came home in March, it was back to the same old stuff.

One Sunday afternoon, we were supposed to go to a party at my friend from work's house. He was drunk, and once again I would have to go alone and make excuses. I had enough. I was tired of stepping on eggshells pretending everything was fine. I was always very careful not to put him down because I was afraid of what he might do to himself. But I was tired of his selfishness and everything he had put me through.

I told him that he was worthless, I had lost all respect for him and I wanted him to leave. I was angry and said a lot of other mean things, all of which were true. I went to my friend's party and pretended everything was fine. When I got home he was gone. It was the middle of April, and he had gone to his mother's in Havertown.

It wasn't but a few days there until he was staying at Sandy's house, who was the woman he had an affair with off and on for a couple of years. He swore they were only friends, and so did she. It didn't matter, I was glad he was out of the house. He still came to the house everyday to see the kids. I was very nice to him because I didn't want anything to happen to him.

A couple of weeks later on Friday, May 3rd he came to the house. He said he wanted to say goodbye to the kids because he was going to kill himself. His court date for the DUI was coming up, and he couldn't stand the thought of going to jail. The lawyer had said that jail time would only be 30 days, tops. This was so ridiculous.

I tried to keep him at the house and stall him. He didn't tell the kids what he was planning. I wasn't sure if it was another threat or if he meant it, but I begged him to get his things and move back home with us. I didn't want him back, but I felt I had no choice. I called his mother and his best friend, and they drove the hour to my house. Huey and I looked all over town for him. We found him at one point, and he was very drunk and refused to get in the car and come home with us. He got in his car and took off.

Billy's birthday was on Sunday, and the whole family was coming over. We waited and waited but Bill never came. I knew he would never miss Billy's birthday. I knew he was dead. I called the police and reported him missing. They said he probably was just away somewhere for the weekend because we were separated. When I told them his credit cards had not been used and that he had made suicide threats, they said they would keep a look out for his car.

I didn't know what to do so I went to work Monday. I hadn't been there long when I got a call from the police that they had found Bill's car in Valley Forge National Park. I called Bill's brother, Bob, and headed home immediately. They used search dogs and found Bill on Mount Misery in Valley Forge. He had shot himself in the head. I could not go identify Bill's body so Bob went. Telling the kids was the hardest thing I have ever done in my life. Billy had just turned 14, Jimmy was 13 and Michael was 11. Our lives would never be the same.

Bill had left a will that he had handwritten. He was adamant that he did not want a funeral. I did look at his arm under the sheet to make sure it was him. I saw the tattoos and the scar on his wrist from that weekend of love that seemed like it was in another lifetime. We had a service for the immediate family at the funeral home with a priest then he was cremated. I felt like everyone probably hated me because there was no funeral, but those were his final wishes, and surprisingly, even his mother agreed. Oddly enough, I felt no guilt. I knew that I did everything I could possibly do. I did feel extreme anger at his selfishness and hurting his family so badly. I went back and forth between anger and uncontrollable sobbing with grief. I missed the man that I once knew and had always hoped would reappear. I didn't miss the paranoid drunk that he had become. I hated that house in Downingtown, which did not have many happy memories, mostly bad, and I wanted to move so badly. The psychiatrist said the children already lost their father, and I shouldn't take them away from their home, school, and friends. He was right. The boys and I had two therapy sessions, and he said we were coping fine and didn't need to come back. I had raised my sons the way I was raised: We moved forward and rarely spoke of it. I had ruined another generation.

In less than two weeks after my husband died, my work called to say another nurse had hurt his back and would be out for a while so they needed me to come back to work. I was numb and not in my right mind, but I was too shell-shocked to argue, so I returned to work. I was able to work part-time because I would get Social Security checks to make up the difference.

It was time for me to get my life together and raise my boys. I looked at my life and the negative beliefs and behavior patterns, and promised myself I would break the cycle of madness. I was determined to find a way to change my life and find true happiness. This would take many years of soul searching and learning about the spiritual pathway and how the Universe worked.

The first step was to discover my negative beliefs and behavior patterns then work on changing them. Here are three areas Louise Hay says are necessary for change:

Nurturing the willingness to let go,
Controlling the mind, and
Learning how forgiveness of self and others releases us.

CHAPTER 8
Creating My Beautiful New Life

66 My Spirit is Free

My spirit is soaring free from ego

Ready to receive all good from the universe

My spirit guides me where ever we go

Excited to practice, learn and rehearse

My spirit is love in all of its forms

No longer restrained by society's norms **99**

~ Jody Kratz

Many of us are drawn to the spiritual path to overcome the various adversities we have encountered in our lives. My husband's suicide in 1996 pushed me to really look at my life and decide what behaviors and thought patterns got me to that point in time.

I discovered that I had followed in the footsteps of my mother and was an enabler. I was surrounded by alcoholics my entire life. I didn't drink after I had children but I attracted needy alcoholics that suffered from depression. I would go from being friend and lover to being a mother figure.

I controlled the lives of my husband and my children. I never let them learn how to be independent and take ownership of their lives. When you let others depend on your power instead of developing their own, you are doing them a big dis-service.

I became aware of the negative beliefs and patterns but it took a long time to really change them. I studied many programs over the years. Since I had an hour drive each way to and from work, I would listen to audio programs while I was in the car. I listened to Wayne Dyer, Carolyn Myss, and Eckhart Tolle, to name a few. I was an Insider's Club member of Nightingale Conant. I would pay the monthly membership fee and buy the courses for shipping only.

I loved the way the courses made me feel while a listening to them, but, unfortunately, once I was out of the car, it was business as usual. They say it takes 30 days for a new habit to become firmly rooted. The problem was that I would listen to one course and start right in on the next one without really putting into practice anything I had learned. I was even worse with books. I would read a few chapters, then another book would catch my eye, and I would start on that book. This went on until my early to mid-forties.

I think you absorb more knowledge than you think and eventually reach the tipping point where you start to make real changes in your life. I also noticed that material comes to you when you are ready to understand it. Very early on my spiritual path, there were two particular books I bought, not because they resonated with me, but because they were best sellers. One was *The Course In Miracles* and the other was *The Power of Now* by Ekhart Tolle.

The *Course in Miracles* might as well have been written in Greek, I didn't understand any of it, so I struggled through a few chapters and gave up. Much later down the road I discovered both books again. This time I was drawn to them, and lo and behold they made perfect sense to me. The more I learned, the more I knew I had to make changes in my life, but I kept getting swept up in the daily grind of my life as it was.

My husband's death in1996 left me feeling lost and alone. Even though the relationship was destroyed long before his death, I think part of me had always hoped that he would go back to being the man I fell in love with so many years before. I just took one day at a time; I was merely existing trying to get through each day.

My children took their father's death better than I could have ever imagined. They had active social lives and many friends. I, on the other hand, felt I didn't belong in Downingtown. My friends and my work were back in Havertown where I grew up. It was an hour away, too far to visit very often. I never would have gotten through the experience if it wasn't for my mother and my best friend, Donna. I would talk to Donna on the phone for hours almost every night. I was beginning to be very lonely and wished I had a man in my life.

I didn't know anything about the law of attraction at the time or how it worked. As an example, let's take money. Were you told, "No you can't have those shoes; we can't afford it," or perhaps it was, "Rich people are selfish and dishonest."

Look at your list of beliefs about money and take the negative beliefs and really examine them to see if they are true for you. Turn the negative thoughts into positive affirmations such as: "I can afford to buy whatever I need and more." "Rich people provide jobs for other people and donate millions of dollars to charities."

You cannot experience prosperity until you examine your negative beliefs about money. You attract what you focus your attention on. If you focus on lack of money, you will have a lack of money.

The law of attraction applies to every area of your life. If you tell yourself, "I hate my job," and focus on everything you don't like about it, you will get more of the same. Even if you took a new position, coming from that mindset you would get more of the same.

The law of attraction is more than hoping and wishing for what you want. It's the same with affirmations. You have to change your beliefs before you can attract what you want into your life. You can say an affirmation everyday such as, "my income steadily increases from sources known and unknown," but it is guaranteed nothing will happen as long as deep down inside you have a belief that having a lot of money is somehow bad.

This is why it is so important to write down your beliefs about every area of your life such as relationships, money, career, and SELF. Really get to the bottom of those negative beliefs and change them. You cannot come from a place of lack when you are trying to attract something into your life. You either will not get it at all, or you will get exactly what you didn't want because you were focusing on the lack of what you wanted.

66 We are what we think...

All that we are,

arises with our thoughts.

With our thoughts

we make our world. **99**

~ Buddha

It seems that everywhere I went I would see couples, and they all seemed so happy. I wanted to have somebody to share my life with. Every night in desperation I would hope and pray for somebody to come into my life. Nothing good is ever manifested out of desperation. I would say to myself "I don't want an alcoholic," and "I want someone who is happy."

Affirmations need to be stated in a positive manner. I was focusing so much on what I didn't want, which was an alcoholic, that I got exactly what I focused my attention on. Another alcoholic! The cycle was about to begin again.

I was about to meet another self-absorbed alcoholic who was not emotionally supportive of me whatsoever. Another man to enable. Another man that went from my lover, to being like a little boy that I had to mother.

My husband died in May of 1996. My well-meaning friends knew I was lonely and tried to encourage me to get out and meet people. They would invite me places, we would go out and it would be fun, but I didn't meet anyone. My friend, Karen, kept telling me about her brother, Mark, and how much fun he was, and that she wanted us to meet. My little inner voice told me no, this isn't the right one. I kept making one excuse after another not to meet him. She even planned a few meetings, and I cancelled at the last minute every time.

She kept up, and finally in January of 1997 I gave in. My inner voice kept saying, "don't go," but I ignored it thinking I couldn't possibly back out again. It would take several more years until I would recognize that the inner voice was my divine guidance.

Mark and I had arranged to meet one night in the bar at a restaurant. Karen and her husband were there, too. I can remember thinking he wasn't really my type. I was usually attracted to short, stocky, dark hair, and dark-eyed men. He was tall, blonde, green eyes, and a great muscular body.

I rarely drank because it makes me so sick. Every year or two I would forget about the two-day hangover and make the mistake of drinking too much. Unfortunately, that turned out to be one of those nights. I was very nervous and thought I would have a few beers to relax. One beer led to another, and the four of us went to a night club. We were all pretty trashed except Karen's husband who was the designated driver.

Mark and I had a strong physical attraction, and we ended up back at his apartment until I was sober enough to drive. He was a gentleman and said I could sleep in his room, and he would sleep on the couch. We drank a few more beers and ended up in his bed. I woke up about 4:30 in the morning sick as hell, looked over at him sleeping and thought: "Oh my God, what have I done?" I got dressed, snuck out of the apartment and went home. I don't know which was worse, the guilt or the hangover. I had not yet learned about the importance of forgiveness. I was good at forgiving others but not myself. I was very hard on myself at that time. I had never just gone out with a man and slept with him the first night. I felt dirty and ashamed. He called me later that day and wanted to come over. I told him no, that I felt too sick. Mark never could take no for an answer, so he came over anyway. He met my sons, who were fine and said they just wanted me to be happy. I was so proud of how loving and supportive they were. Mark stayed over and slept on the couch.

Things went very well the first few months. I explained to him that I would never be with an alcoholic again. He said that he only drank socially. He started bringing his son and daughter with him to visit after a few months. I had a four-bedroom home, so two of my sons would sleep in the same room, and his kids would stay in a room. We met in January, and by the end of June he was staying at my house most of the time with his kids. He shared custody and had them every other week.

My inner voice was again telling me that he was not the one, and that five children were just too much for me, but I didn't know how to get myself out of the situation. I decided to take my kids to the beach for a week, and he somehow talked me into bringing his kids with me, even though he had to work. I just wanted to be alone with my kids. But he went with us and drove two hours each way to work and back to the shore.

I still wasn't over my husband's death and was very confused. I was not good at saying no and setting boundaries at that point in my life. It is so important to learn how to say no and stick to it. You should never let other people take your energy. It took me almost eight more years to learn about personal power or energy and not to give it away.

> **66** You give your power away when
> you make someone or something
> outside of you more important
> than what is inside of you. **99**
> ~ *Alan H. Cohen*

The middle of August that year I got the shock of my life. We had been seeing each other for seven months when out of the blue, he showed up on my doorstep saying he had been evicted from his apartment. My inner voice was screaming now. He said he didn't pay the rent because he knew he was going to end up living with me anyway.

I was just sick to my stomach. I had no intention of asking him to move in; he just assumed that was how it was going to be. I told him he could stay with me until he found a place. I didn't see how he could live with me when he had his children every other week and they were enrolled in first and second grade in a school an hour away.

He said he would like to have full custody of the children, but their mother wouldn't go for that, so he would just see them on weekends. I think he knew all along she would give them up in a heartbeat. So, suddenly, there he was with all of his things moving in. The kids were there with us in August because he said there was no sense sending them to their mother's house just to be put in daycare.

He was so pushy and overbearing, and I didn't seem able to speak up enough. He would only hear what he wanted to hear. I tried to tell him this wasn't going to work with the kids. I don't know why I was surprised when their mother said they could live with him full time. I had never even met her or talked to her. She had never been to our house and had no idea where we lived. She sent her children to live with a total stranger in a neighborhood she knew nothing about. He signed them up for school against my weak protests, and it was a done deal.

It was crowded with four boys and one girl. I had a basement that wasn't finished but it had windows, a beautiful fireplace, and a separate entrance. I had 25,000 dollars from my husband's life insurance, and I spent it all to finish the basement. It was beautiful. There were two bedrooms and a full bathroom, and a living room with a fireplace. My two oldest sons couldn't wait to move down there. They were ages 14 and 15. Great, now my savings were gone, and I had a six bedroom, three and a half bathroom home to keep clean.

Mark was a big talker and said that with both our salaries I would have a maid when he moved in. Well there was no way with five children that we had the money for a maid since I was only working three 8-hour shifts one week and two 8-hour shifts the next week, and I was also getting Social Security checks for the boys. I ended up having to work three 12-hour shifts to make ends meet.

My life had turned into a nightmare, and I could see no way out of the situation. I was working 36 hours a week; and doing all of the house work and laundry. I wouldn't get home from work until about one in the morning and I would get up at 6 a.m. to get the kids off to school. I would try to take a nap but I worked 12-hour shifts and had to be back at work at 11 a.m. So add exhaustion to all of the other issues.

I was very good at manifesting money and promotions at work. I didn't know about the law of attraction at the time. It worked in that area of my life because I had no negative thoughts surrounding money or job performance. I just focused on what I wanted and had no doubt it would come to me. In fact, I doubled my income in nine years from 2001 to 2010. But at home, things kept going downhill after Mark moved in. His social drinking became an everyday thing. I found out that he would go to the bar at lunch while he was working. When he was pulled over for making an illegal right turn on a red light while I was with him, I discovered that he had a suspended driver's license from a prior DUI! I was now stuck with a drunk and a liar. The fine was $1,500, and there would be three of those fines in the first two years.

We went on a cruise in the fall of 1997, and he proposed to me on stage in front of all of those people and gave me the Tanzanite ring surrounded by diamonds that I had put on my credit card that day. He said he wanted to buy it for me, and if I charged it, he would pay me back.

How do you say no to a proposal when you are onstage in front of all those people? I was furious at him for putting me in that position. I told him we may be engaged, but there was no way I was getting married. There would be two more rings at the next two Christmases. He paid for half of one ring out of the three.

We had a joint bank account and joint credit cards. He would give me his whole paycheck, and then buy whatever he wanted for himself and his kids. The debt was really adding up. His car died within the first year we were together. I gave him my car and bought a new one.

He traded that in the next year for a used pickup truck. The truck was in my name because he still didn't have a driver's license. I justified it to myself because he had to get to work, or I would be supporting all of us, and we were too far in debt. The truck ended up being totaled in yet another DUI for which he ended up going to jail for 60 days. He was on work release so there was still money coming in.

I had to take care of the five children by myself for two months. His kids' mother would only take the kids every other weekend because she said she had a life to live. What about my life?

I finally started wising up. I separated our money – no more joint bank account or joint credit cards. He gave me $300 a week and complained about it. I still paid all of the bills, utilities, mortgage, food, and clothes for all five children. I was paying off the credit cards that he ran up before

I took his name off the accounts. I let him get another truck in my name again because of our financial situation. We had been together about four or five years by this time.

Things were really becoming wild in the house. I took a job as a nursing supervisor because it was a big pay increase. It was Monday through Friday, 3p.m. to 11p.m. I was the on-site administrator at the hospital. My sons were now in their teens and were also drinking. I didn't know it at the time but Mark was buying them beer. What a stand up guy. He also let them smoke cigarettes. I figured that out and asked him how would he like it if I let his kids smoke? On the weekends, the teenagers would be drunk, he would be drunk, and it was a nightmare. His son would get so frightened he would go sleep in the room with his sister.

They were always getting into fights. I asked him to move out several times but he said he would send his children back to their mother. I felt like those children were my own by that time. I wanted to keep the kids and have him move out. He used them to keep me under his thumb.

One time he was out Christmas shopping in his truck and then must have gone to the bar. I was wondering where he was when I got a phone call from the police saying they found his truck slammed in a tree with no one in it. I was so angry but I had no idea where he was. I went in the dining room for some reason, and there he was, passed out on the floor having urinated on himself. That's how drunk he was, and to think of him driving made me sick.

He tried to get my youngest son to say he was driving and was scared when he got in the accident so he ran from the scene. I told him to man up and take responsibility for his own actions. How dare he try to get my son to take the rap for him? I decided he had to go. He said I couldn't keep the children, and I said "fine, then send them to their mother's house." She never signed them up for school, and they missed a week or two. Needless to say, they all ended up back with me.

Mark spent 90 days in jail while I took care of everything. I told him he would never drive another vehicle of mine again. His friends had to drive him to work. He stopped drinking when he got out of jail but that didn't last for long.

I began listening to spiritual audio programs on my two-hour commute sometime around the year 2001. I must have listened to hundreds over the years. It was finally starting to sink in little by little.

Between my sons' drinking and Mark's drinking, things just kept getting worse. He would fight with the boys a lot, then the next day they would be buddies. He worked in masonry, and he was a big man. Luckily they were usually able to out run him. One night he and my son Jimmy got into a fight. I guess Jimmy got tired of running, and he whacked Mark in the head with a board. Mark was dazed and had a huge gash above his right eye; then he was like a raging bull.

His son called the police because he was so afraid his dad would kill Jimmy. The police came and took them both to jail. I paid the bail and picked both of them up the next morning. They walked out laughing and like best friends again. I was disgusted. I wanted him out so badly, but he wouldn't leave. I was desperate to get out of this situation.

The insanity went on until early 2007. He was drunk one night, and I decided to try and push him over the edge then call the police to get him out. I was raised to be an enabler and knew better than to mess with a drunk. That is probably why he never hit me in all of those years. He would break things and punch walls and doors, but he never hit me.

I was in the kitchen screaming and yelling at him trying to get him angry. He was punching the cabinets, and he took my can of Pepsi and poured it in my purse. His back was to the kitchen sliding door. Things were really starting to escalate. He was so drunk he didn't notice my oldest son, Bill, come in the door. Bill had a gun and a license to carry.

He had his gun out and said, "Stop it right now, Mom. Don't make me do this." I saw by the look in Bill's eyes that he was serious. I just stopped and walked away. Mark never knew that Bill was behind him with the gun. I also found out at the time that he had been doing Cocaine for quite awhile. This was a new low for him. I was stronger by this time and kicked him out in early February of 2007. He went to live in a rooming house next to a bar, of course. He had one tiny room with a bathroom. His children stayed with me. He was like a lost child.

I was very good at forgiveness, and we remained friends. I would pick him up and take him grocery shopping or to run errands. We would go to dinner sometimes. I guess we were too friendly looking back. He hurt his back in May 2007 and was unable to work. He needed surgery. He wanted to move back in with me.

My little inner voice was now my big inner voice. I understood it was my intuition and that I needed to follow it. Jimmy and Bill had moved out of the house by that time, and I am ashamed to admit that once again I ignored my intuition. I told him he could live in the basement until he got on his feet.

He was a nightmare. He was out of work getting small workers' compensation checks while his case was waiting to go to court. I couldn't get him out, I was stuck again. Then, in January of 2008, I found out he was doing Cocaine again. He was drinking as much as ever.

I told him I was done, that I was going to start on-line dating, and he had to go. He tried everything to get me to let him stay. He said he would give me his whole worker's compensation settlement if I would let him live in the basement the rest of his life. Was he out of his mind? The rest of his life? He was 47, and I was about to turn 48!

I had finally come into my own power. I told him he had to go, and it was over for good. I helped him find an apartment but with his criminal record and bad credit, his name couldn't even be on the lease. I wanted him out bad enough that I put the lease in my name only. Everyone said I was crazy and would end up stuck with his rent. I didn't care, I just wanted him out. He paid most of the rent, and I helped him out here and there. He met a woman at the apartments within a few months. I was finally free at last! We remained friends, and the children stayed with me.

It is now March, 2011 and I have been on an incredible journey. I have undergone a complete transformation. I started with looking at my life and discovering the negative patterns and beliefs, then I went on to learning about self-love and self-forgiveness and many other things.

The most important thing in life is to love yourself for who you are right now in this moment. If you can do that, every area of your life will improve. Even if your life isn't going great at the moment, don't put yourself down. Acknowledge and give yourself credit for doing the best that you can at this point in time.

Louise Hay is a big proponent of mirror work. Go to the mirror now and look into your eyes, and say: "I love you." If you have never done mirror work, this is most likely very difficult for you, if not impossible. You are probably looking in the mirror and saying: "My hair is a mess," or "I have bags under my eyes." All kinds of negative thoughts come to mind, maybe even thoughts like "How can I love myself when I'm such a …. " You fill in the blank. I'm sure you can come up with a million reasons not to love yourself.

The trick is to find the reasons why you should love yourself. Stop the negative self talk. Every time you catch yourself thinking negative self thoughts, stop the thought immediately, and replace it with a new positive thought. You have to work in increments so it is believable to your mind. You can't have the thought, "I'm a terrible mother," and replace it with "I'm the best mother in the world." That doesn't work. You have to raise the level of your thoughts in increments that your mind can accept. How about: "I may not be the perfect mother, but I'm doing the best I can and will continue to do better."

Esther and Jerry Hicks point out in their Abraham works that people vibrate at different levels. You can only attract things that are at the same vibration as yourself. They also say you have to raise your vibration in increments.

Your vibrations can differ in the different areas of your life. You may not have issues surrounding money, therefore your thoughts surrounding money are at a high vibration level and you probably have the money you need and then some. At the same time, you may have negative thoughts about love and relationships, which put you at a lower vibration level, and you probably are in a relationship that is not at all satisfying, or not in a relationship at all.

That is why it is so important to look at *every* area of your life and examine your thoughts and beliefs. Keep the positive thoughts and change the negative thoughts.

Part of loving yourself is making sure you do things to satisfy you. You may think this is selfish at first; believe me, it isn't. When you use all of your energy taking care of everyone but you, it doesn't usually have a very good outcome. You feel tired and drained most of the time, and eventually you become physically ill. That is your spirit giving you a time out. You cannot help others when you are physically and emotionally spent.

So. the best way to serve others is to take care of you first. Try to do something for yourself every day, even if it is as simple as a bubble bath at the end of a long day. Don't ever let anyone make you feel guilty about doing things to make yourself happy. Guilt is another thing in your life that has to go. Louise Hay says, "Resentment, guilt, and fear cause more problems than anything else."

The first step in loving yourself is to let go of the past. Letting go of the past involves forgiveness of yourself and others. This can be very difficult. You have to find a way to truly forgive those who have hurt you in the past and forgive yourself for mistakes you have made or for hurting others. It is the only way to move forward.

There have been entire books written on the subject of forgiveness; you need to do a little research and find a method that works for you. If there is a person in particular that you are having a hard time forgiving, write a letter to that person and lay it all out. Don't hold back. After you have written the letter, take it out in the yard and burn it saying something like: "I forgive you and release you from my mind and life with love."

You can't change the past it is over and done, so get over it. We all have our "story," you know, the one we tell over and over to anyone who will listen about how we have been wronged in the past. That is a victim mentality and as long as you see yourself as a victim you will continue to be a victim and will attract more of the same to your life. Stop playing the victim now and take responsibility for your own life.

You can't change another person's behavior or opinion, but you can change the way you react to them. As long as you relive this story over and over, you are giving all of your power to people and things in the past. Your power is in the present moment. We create our future from the present moment, so make this and every moment to come a positive one.

You get back what you give out. So make sure what you are projecting out into the world is what you want to receive. If you criticize others, expect to be criticized. If you are kind to others, they will be kind to you. Let's talk more about living in the present moment.

How often are you really present in the moment and enjoying life as it unfolds? Or is your mind on old stuff from the past which you can never change anyway? Maybe your mind is in the future dreading something you're not even sure will happen.

Most of our fears are all in our head. How often is your life really in danger in the present moment? Okay there are those rare instances, but for the most part , it is our mind fearing some future event. Trust in the process of life; live happily aware in the present moment and everything will unfold as it was meant to be.

I'm not suggesting that you don't make plans for the future; just try not to dwell on the future and let life pass you by. How many times have you said "I'll be happy when... I get the better job, the bigger house, the perfect mate," or whatever it is you tell yourself?

I've got news for you: Happiness comes from within. Happiness does not follow material things, it's quite the opposite, material things follow happiness. Find a way to be happy with yourself and your life exactly the way they are in this moment, and your life will improve more and more each day that passes.

Remember, you create your future from the present moment, and if you can be in a state of happiness and gratitude, then by the law of attraction, your life will improve. When you find your mind stuck too long in the past or future, bring it back to the present moment. Everyday think of things you are grateful for even if it is as simple as a great parking space. The more gratitude you bring into your life the better you feel.

Make it a point everyday to compliment people even if it is just: "Your hair looks nice." Watch how a simple compliment can make another person glow, and notice how good that makes you feel. It's all about feeling good in the moment.

I have polished stones each with a different word on it. I will pick a stone for the day and put it in my pocket. When I carry my stone that has gratitude written on it, every time I reach into my pocket I think of something I am grateful for in my life. This really works and it makes you feel good.

I decided sometime during 2009 that I wanted to make my living doing some kind of spiritual work but I wasn't sure what that would be. I would say the same affirmation every day: "My income is ever increasing from sources known and unknown. I live a happy, beautiful life and work per diem so I can see my friends at the hospital."

Affirmations work but not always in the way you think they should work. Sometimes the Universe has a different take on your affirmations. I saw an advertisement on the Hay House website for training to become a Heal Your Life® licensed workshop leader/teacher. My intuition said "You have to do this."

I thought it very strange. I had thought I would make money investing in real estate, and someday eventually be able to work per diem for fun and write spiritual books. I had never given a thought to workshops or being a speaker. I had read all of Sonia Choquette's books by this point and knew I had to follow my intuition.

I saw the Heal Your Life ® advertisement in May, 2010. I had already signed up to go to Chicago in November to work with Sonia Choquette to get my sixth sensory level one certification. The Heal Your Life® Teacher certification was a week in San Diego in September.

My intuition said sign up now. These days, I always follow my intuition now no matter how crazy it seems. Sonia calls it living from the heart. I have tamed my ego enough not to allow those negative thoughts to interfere. But my ego was chattering: "How can you afford both trips? What makes you think you can teach anybody anything?"

I told my ego to shut up and signed up for the training. I was going completely on intuition and faith. You have to have faith that the Universe or God has a plan and everything works out the way it is supposed to when you listen to your spirit.

I would go to work every day grateful and happy with my life as it was; knowing that bigger and better things were coming my way. I would enter the hospital and repeat my affirmation. I would think to myself that I won't be here much longer, and I really should start organizing my office and throwing things out. You have to say your affirmations and feel as though it's already done.

I went to the Heal Your Life® training that September, and it was awesome. I experienced such growth. I was so excited to get started on my new career path. I knew it would take time to build the business but I had a very high paying job at the hospital in the meantime.

I was called to the Vice President of Nursing's office on October 4th, 2010. I knew the hospital was laying people off, and I was concerned about my 50 employees. They were fine. I was the one that was laid off. I had worked there for 23 years with not a spot on my record. We were all devastated. I understood the reason; it was done by job description.

I cried my eyes out on my way home. I had just mortgaged my two rental properties against my own home in the spring. I had paid cash for them with lines of credit from my own home. I couldn't get them mortgaged when the economy crashed because they were bought under my corporate name. I had rolled all the variable rate lines of credit into one 15-year mortgage at 4.5%. Now, I had a whopping monthly mortgage payment and no job.

I had already paid for my sixth sensory training with Sonia in November but that didn't include airfare and hotel. My spirit told me stop worrying, everything will be fine. This layoff is a blessing and a gift from God. Deep in my heart I knew this to be true. But my ego got to me for about two weeks.

I was on the phone day and night talking to my friends at work going on and on about my "story," even though I knew better than to get caught up in that nonsense. It doesn't accomplish anything, and you can't change the past.

The Director of Human Resources at the hospital called me about a job he heard about at a nursing home. He was so kind and caring that I didn't want to say no. I went to the nursing home, and it was a patient care manager job, which would be a pay cut. My intuition said, "no this isn't for you," and I turned down the job offer. It had only been two weeks.

My family was a little upset, but I explained I had a six-month severance package of full pay and benefits. I told them I could afford to wait for a better job. Money seemed to be rolling in. I had about 240 vacation hours they paid me, and I still got my large manager bonus in November. I also get unemployment benefits.

I did my sixth sensory certification, and it changed my life forever. I never understood how to fully connect with my spirit and guides until that training. I started a daily meditation practice that has caused such a shift in me. I had meditated over the years but never made it a practice.

Part of my severance package was being sent to an elite firm that helps you with job transition. They have so many resources and classes. I took them all and was particularly focused on entrepreneurship classes for my new business. I took everything but resume writing.

I just couldn't bring myself to go back to the daily grind. My former employer sent me a job openings list every week. I only called about jobs I wasn't qualified for. I just grew happier every day. You would think I would be getting nervous and unhappy as time went by since I wasn't employed. It was just the opposite.

I signed up for more advanced training classes. I went to Sedona, Arizona in February, 2011 to become a Licensed Heal Your Life® personal coach. I love the idea of working with people one-on-one to create the lives they've always dreamed of.

Then I was given this wonderful opportunity to be part of this book from one of my new friends, Lisa Hardwick. I had always dreamed of being an author and said affirmations but it wasn't even on my mind. My life is coming together perfectly.

I just returned from a weekend Sonia Choquette workshop on working with your guides. It is March 17th, 2011, and my severance runs out the end of April. I am doing my sixth sensory level two certification in April. I have signed up to train to be a coach for "Calling in the One." I would love to help people find their soul mates.

I am being coached myself by beautiful Nachhi. She is another gift from the Universe. She does prosperity coaching, and she is helping me build my business from the ground up.

My family is fit to be tied because I'm not even trying to find a job. They are convinced I've lost my mind. I still haven't made a resume, and I'm not planning to either. I have no doubt that everything is coming together in Divine order, and I am doing what I was meant to do in this life time. I am loving every second of my beautifully restored new life!

CAROL ROESE

Chapter 9:
My Adventured Life

CHAPTER 9
My Adventured Life

Even when I have experienced some bad moments along my path, I always had a great feeling about life. I usually think to myself, "It is totally fine, Caroline. This is just happening for a reason and something better is coming." I can even be in the middle of total despair and still feel confident that the good and new are coming on my way. We all have unpleasant situations in our journey. We have to be strong enough to take responsibility for our beliefs, actions, ideas and change what is needed.

I remember when I was young, I had a horrible feeling about when my dad or my mom would finish their journey in this lifetime. I still have the vivid memories of crying while imagining how I would suffer when my parents died. I realized that I was spending a lot of energy on something that was impossible to know when it was going to happen. Imagine if I passed my whole life thinking about that, and I leave the planet earlier than them, or perhaps I have a different view of life and death by the time something happens.

My dad was diagnosed with lung cancer few years ago, and I went through a period of suffering, crying almost constantly every single day, becoming stressed about the situation. I even thought about moving back to Brazil to be close to him, but my life was already established here in America.

I tried to help him change his mind and his thoughts, but my dad was very obstinate. He used to say that every person has an expiration date in this world and his was already ending. I went to Brazil many times, sometimes even twice a year to spend time with him. I used to go just to spoil him and do whatever he wanted, I pleased him as much as I could.

I think the best thing I ever did was to stop suffering in advance. I realized that constantly crying would make him feel bad, and he never wanted us worrying about him. I made the decision that I was going to cry only when something happened, and I had a feeling anyway that he was going to live many, many years. So imagine suffering five or maybe ten years in a row and nothing happened? What a lot of wasted energy in my life – and also in his life, because I believe we transmit the vibration of what we're thinking to the people we are thinking about.

Anyway, God and my dad decided that was time for him to rest, and I don't question that decision. God knows exactly what He does. I have my days that I cry, because I miss his hugs, his kisses, his laugh, his jokes, but I know he is with me every single day. I think I handled the situation very well, and it was not even close to what I thought when I was young.

My message to you is, do not suffer in advance for something that you do not know is even going to happen. It might happen, but in a way that you can be comfortable with and have a better understanding about the whole situation.

I had a great childhood, we used to play all kind of games that we kids invented. We were very creative and had lots of fun. I am the youngest child with three older brothers. In general, we have a happy family. All of my experiences are stepping stones to where I am right now, and to what I will be in the future. Now, when I have moments that upset me, I understand and don't let them bother me, because I know that these moments are stepping stones into a better life.

When I was eighteen years old, things were not so good. My life was in a time of manipulation, jealousy and disagreements. Five years later, desperation and depression were becoming a part of me. I started asking myself:

"Why do I have to be in this situation? Should I just leave the planet right now? What am I suppose to do here? Am I designed to suffer? Do I have to spend my life in this hell? And what if the people making me feel this way, leave the planet now?"

I was completely lost, sad, grumpy, and resentful. If I had the wisdom that I have now, knowing that we have the power to change our lives, I would never have gotten to that point. Remember when I say, we can always learn a lesson from good and bad situations.

I was told about a very good psychologist and advised to talk with her. Maybe she would be able to help me. But I was completely broke and could not afford to go. So, I decided to talk to my dad. I explained to him that I really needed some help, and he said he was able to pay for my sessions. Deal! That was a great sign. When we really desire something, the Universe is in charge of getting what we want.

So I began the treatment with the psychologist. The time required varies from person to person, but in my case, I was ready to move on with my life in four months. The best part of all of this was that during the sessions, the psychologist introduced to me the art of embracing my life, where you can achieve anything you desire.

Imagine thirteen years ago, someone from the countryside, raised as Catholic, discovering all about this new way of living her life. It was an enormous revelation. The psychologist introduced me to the technique of writing down what you want to happen in your life. So, that is exactly what I did. From my list, I remembered I asked for a car, a foreign trip and a computer. These were my three major desires, I do not even remember the rest.

But the interesting thing is that at that moment I was completely broke. I had no idea whatsoever how I could make those things happen, but they came to my life in ways that I did not even plan. Remember, when we desire something we just need to focus on the results, on exactly what we want. The how's are the Universe's business. At the time, I was not aware of the power that all we have but never claim, but it was a great beginning.

When I was around 10 years old, my grandfather used to read books about the power of our mind, and my mother used to think he was completely crazy. Well, it is quite understandable, it was a very different approach to life. In my early 20's, I read some books by Louise Hay and also an author from Brazil, Lauro Trevisan.

When we are young, we do not have much focus on healing, or taking care of ourselves, all we want is to get things going. Although I had great opportunities for awakening the power to heal ourselves and attract what we want, at that time I did not take advantage of it. I believe things happen in a Divine order and now, I trust that. If I would have used all the techniques that I now know about how to attract what you want in your life, I am very sure my life today would be on a totally different page. I have all the time in the world to get and do what I desire.

The depression and desperation that took place in my life years ago, transformed itself into a desire to move on to a totally new and different life for myself. Since I was young, I had it in my mind that my hometown had a small-town mentality. I always had a different outlook of life. Sometimes, I even have deep contradictions inside of me.

I had the desire to live somewhere people can think, dress or be whoever they want without being judged. I also had the desire to move on with my life, do something different and to take risks. All these decisions together brought me to the United States nine years ago.

I am very thankful for all the strength I developed over all these years. Even in the moments that my life has been painful, I seldom had the feeling of giving up. I was able to understand that this was just a time that

I needed to learn. I guess I still do.

I would describe myself as someone who is always able to learn something new, which brings more joy to my life. I see myself as someone continuously changing and learning. I like to see myself growing and adding many different ways of living a healthier and more awakened life. My first years in the United States were very challenging for me, even though I knew the language well enough to communicate. Many times, I felt frustrated, sad and shy because I needed someone to help me in every single step I took. My mom raised all of her kids to be very independent, so needing someone to help with most of the things I wanted was very difficult for me. But I knew I could survive, and I did.

I lived in San Diego for almost five years, which was a great experience. In the beginning, I was frequently frustrated – which is totally normal when someone starts a new adaptation process. After all, it was a completely different country, language, culture, and people. Even though most of my friends were Brazilian, the hard times were still there.

It took me nearly three years to get totally adapted to the system and to the people. But the last two years in California, I felt totally peaceful and in harmony. Even though I did not have many worries, something inside of me was saying that I needed to move on. The feeling that I could do much better kept ringing.

From the time I moved to San Diego, I had been working as a waitress and a babysitter. Nothing against to these jobs, I was grateful to be employed. But for someone who has a Bachelor's degree and speaks three languages, I felt I could do much more for me and for others.

During the time I was in California, I had gone to Miami twice for my birthday. I really liked Miami. It was fun and had a Latin environment – I kind of felt at home, like in Brazil. By the way, it also looks more like my country than the U.S.

So three years ago, I decided to give it a shot and try to find myself; who I am, what are my desires, what do I want to do in my life, what is my purpose – so I moved to Miami. I love anything related to music whether it is dancing or singing or both. In my mind, Miami was the perfect place to be involved with music, or whatever else would come to me.

One of my friends told me that the reason I chose Miami to find myself, was because in the name MIAMI comes the words I AM. That is exactly what happened to me, I have been in Miami for three years, and I can say I have found my passion in life, and I am very excited and enthusiastic about it.

When I got to Florida, I started working as a waitress. But being tired of this kind of job, I decided to build my resume. Since my Bachelor's degree in Brazil is in Accounting, and I had over 10 years' experience in Brazil as an Accountant, I wanted to apply for a job in the accounting field. I thought would be easier for me to get into this career again since I am a very good accountant with a lot of good experience. But for some reason I never found a job in this field, and again, I am very grateful for it.

It was around this time I got back to reading self-help books. I had been interested in these types of books in Brazil, and also, while I was living in San Diego, I read many books by Louise Hay. That is where I started my real awakening process.

I remember when I announced to my friends and co-workers in San Diego that I was moving to Miami, they all asked me the same questions: Do you have a job there waiting for you? Do you have a place to live there? How are you going to deal with a new city? Do you have friends there? My answers were all the same: I am completely fine, I do not have job, nor a place to live, nor friends. But I trust everything is all right, and I am going in the right direction.

I always have this voice inside of me guiding me to the right way.   Later I found that was my inner guidance or my intuition talking to me, and I learned to trust it. When I follow my intuition, I never regret it.

In Miami, I was feeling unmotivated waiting tables, and I could not get any job in the Accounting field. One day my manager was sick and could not work. The general manager asked who was working as a waitress or waiter that day, and since I was the veteran, he asked me if I would fill in as manager that day. To my surprise, he started asking me to fill in as manager more and more often, then also asked me to work in different restaurants of the company.

I ended up working as a floater manager where I was covering all the days when managers in all the restaurants of the company would call in sick and for vacations. I did that for awhile, and when the busy season came, I decided to go back to work as a waitress.

But after three months working as a waitress again, I decided that I needed a change. If I was tired of being a waitress before, how could I possibly came back to do exactly the same thing? Now I can see very clearly, once again, that everything happens for a reason. When a person is experiencing a not-so-comfortable situation, we feel grumpy and sad, however, once things start moving forward and get into the right place, we feel much better.

I considered being a restaurant manager again, but on the other hand, I was embarrassed to ask the general manager. Remember, I was a restaurant manager before and then I requested to go back as a waitress. But three months later, I decided that being a manager was what I really wanted.

I was very shy and hesitant to expose my feelings to the general manager by saying that I really wanted the position back. But I took a deep breath and asked for a little bit of his time because I had something to ask him. He listened to all I said, and told me he would consider it and would give me a call.

I had already done everything I could do, so I decided to work on my affirmations and visualizations. I remembered when I talked to him it was around February. The whole month of March every day during my shifts at work as a waitress, I would write numerous times: "I bless my current job with love, and I release it right now for a much better position as restaurant manager."

I used to write it so much that my co-workers would always ask me what I was doing. I'll never forget the day I was writing my affirmations, and one of my co-worker asked me what I writing. Instead of saying that I was writing my affirmations, my answer was that I was writing a book. I didn't want to have to explain or give them the chance to ruin my goals with their comments or bad energy.

Did you notice what I said: I "was writing a book"? Well, that is exactly what I am doing now; and just by saying it even jokingly, guess what? It is happening right now. That is why I usually tell people to be careful with what you say because it can become your reality. I am proof of that. Also, we need to pay attention to the way we say it, knowing exactly what we want and which way we want it to happen.

I remember back in San Diego, I had to work my last Christmas and New Year's Eve there. In the restaurant business, it is required to work on all holidays. But I said to myself, "Next year I do not care what happens, I will spend the December holidays with my family in Brazil, since I have not spent any one with them in almost five years."

What came to be my reality was that my dad found out he had lung cancer six months after I said I wanted to spend the holidays with my family in Brazil. I ended up going to Brazil to spend the holidays with my family, Because I did not know how long my dad would be alive, my manager could not say no, because it was for an emergency.

What I want to point out is that when you ask something of the Universe, do it in the right way. The way I did it by saying "I do not care what happens," was not the right affirmation. I went to Brazil to spend the holidays with my family, but not for a good reason.

After all my affirmations and visualizations, a couple of friends told me that I should talk to the general manager again while I had the chance, because they were hiring a lot of new managers. Again, I trusted my intuition, and in the power of affirmations, and at the end of March, he made a proposal to me.

He offered the position of full-time manager of one of the biggest restaurants of the company! He advised me that it was a big responsibility, that it was not an easy job, that I would have to manage a lot of employees, and that there was a lot of work to do. My answer again was, I can do it. So I was starting a new cycle of my life in the beginning of April.

This position of manager of this specific restaurant was offered to many people, including experienced managers. They were all afraid to take this job because in their mind they created a monster. They saw the restaurant as too much to handle. First of all, the main office of the corporation was in the same building which meant that every day the general manager and the owners are all there. Also, besides this restaurant, there is another restaurant of the same company where the manager is very competitive, and everyone says this person has very negative energy to work with. My intention on facing this whole situation was to remain calm, and anytime people came to me trying to frighten me about all the danger that could possibly come my way, my answer was all the same: This person, or this situation, does not have power over me. I trust myself, and I know I CAN DO IT.   And, all I can say is that it was one of the best things I have done since I moved to the U.S.

First I had to overcome my fear to commit to such a huge responsibility. To better explain, we usually have to work a very tough schedule, to the point where you have no time to do anything for yourself. I did not have time for socializing because by the time I got home in the evening, I was so exhausted that I did not have enough energy to do anything else. I used to go right to sleep to prepare myself for the next day. I did not have weekends off, and I did not have any flexibility in my schedule. As a good

Sagittarius, I love freedom, feeling free.

Other than that, I learned how to trust myself and believe that I could do a great job as a manager. I wanted to be a different kind of manager where I could nourish my employees, make them feel comfortable, confident, and most importantly, make them feel that they were there to make money, have fun, and be happy.

So every day I wrote lots of affirmations related to my job and posted them on my bedroom wall, or wrote over and over again at work. When I was finished, I would tear them up into pieces, say a prayer and put it all in the trash. For me that ritual was kind of letting go of all my worries and trusting in what would come.

My affirmations were like, " My bosses love me, they appreciate my job, they are very proud of me." I heard over and over again other managers complaining about their bosses, and eventually, they became my bosses also. Because they were always on top of the sales, the pressure on the other managers was extremely high.

In my case, for the whole time I was manager of that specific restaurant, remember one of the toughest of the whole company, I never heard any complaints from any of my bosses, or any pressure about anything – not on sales, not on the way I was managing the employees, not on the way I was handling big events and holidays. Actually the total opposite, the general manager used to say that he was really proud of my job, that he really liked the way I talked and managed the staff, the sales were really good. For this to happen, there must be something really special because he generally does not make any of these comments to anybody else.

Another affirmation I used to write was related to sales: "We are selling a lot; our sales are constantly increasing; our customers are very happy; we all take good care of our guests; our restaurant has a great energy; we make a great deal of sales, and the employees make a great deal of money; we are all blessed."

Another important point of this type of company is that the restaurants are all outdoors. So, if we can attract some people to the restaurant, it attracts other people. People attract other people. If the restaurant is empty when people pass by, they automatically think that there is something wrong with the restaurant, or the food is not good, or service is bad and so on.

We had experienced times that we did not have people in the restaurant. So I started visualizing customers seated on the tables, spending money, being happy. One day I decided to create an experience. I called in everyone from the staff of that specific shift and told them that I was going to teach them something very precious. And also, I told them they could learn this technique and use it for themselves in their personal life and goals.

Then I explained to them that if we continue complaining because we do not have customers, if we keep saying the restaurant is empty, or talking about the bad weather, or lack of money, or lack of sales, we were going to continue to attract more and more of the same. I asked them to go outside and start visualizing customers at their tables, visualize food and drinks on the table, think about their high sales, blessing the great deal of money they were making and then they would see a totally different reality.

Guess what happened that specific day? When we started, we were completely empty. Within no more than five minutes, one table of people sat down, right after another one, and so on. After twenty minutes, we had a lot of people in the restaurant, and we did not have to worry about that for the rest of that day.

I see clearly in my mind one of the waitresses coming to me and saying that it was amazing, it was a miracle. My answer was, of course it is a miracle, it is energy. If you keep complaining and just talking about your problems you just attract more and more problems.

When I started working as a manager I had a meeting every single day with the staff. I can see now that it was practice for what I am doing right now, which is leaving behind this fear of talking to a lot of people at the same time. I discovered that I love to help people to find new ways of living a happier life, and I felt very rewarded when they came to me and said I was making a difference in their lives.

In the meetings, I used to tell them how being grateful for anything in their lives would make a big difference. They used to complain all the time if the customers did not leave any gratuity for them, or if the customer didn't spend enough money in food or drinks so their check would be high and, of course, their tip would be proportional.

When I listened to those kinds of comments, I used to tell them not to worry about it, you are going to be okay at the end of the day. Do not focus on the lack of the tips, or lack of sales because you are going to attract more of "lack-ness." Be grateful for whatever amount of tips you make, be grateful for your customers, be thankful for any sales you make, because you are going to receive more tips, your sales are going to increase, you are going to attract more pleasant customers. Use the words THANK YOU over and over again, then you are going to receive more and more abundance in any area and everything you want in your life.

Another thing I would love to share with you is, we have a tendency to think that if we give someone something, or if we do a favor for somebody, we expect something from that specific person in return. What I believe is important is for us to keep a positive vibrational field around us so we make ourselves and others feel better, then we will automatically receive something good in return.

I remember one day that I had a meeting with my personnel at work where I was explaining to them the importance of being nice to our customers and our co-workers. One of the busboys told me that he was always nice to the waiters and customers, but in return they were not receiving extra tips. I shared my beliefs about giving and not thinking about something in return. Giving is just a good energy that you maintain for yourself, and by maintaining this vibration you receive goodies from everywhere, not only from co-workers.

I used to explain to them that an easy form of understanding would be like if they helped their co-workers not thinking in receiving something specific from them, they might receive something good from their wives, or perhaps they would attract a new beautiful and kind girlfriend, or maybe when they would find a gift from someone when they got home. There are many possibilities when you are in a positive and good vibration.
I try as much as I can to be nice to people and to the world in general, giving what I can, and always when I need something, the Universe provides it for me. I do not even have to sweat it. It is just because I cultivate this positive energy around me.

Over all, I know I did a great job in the restaurant as manager. I am not saying that I was able to do all of this just because of the affirmations. What I am suggesting is that by making the affirmations daily and keeping my vibration in a positive way, it makes a huge difference in my life. I can relax more, and I can enjoy more without stressing myself out, and so can you.

I knew that the manager job was just a stepping stone on my path, and I was also aware that my calling was for a much higher purpose. I found out that a position was available in the office as an administrative assistant. I thought it was a great opportunity for me because I would have a lot more free time and a more flexible schedule so I could start my business on the side. Also, I would be doing something in which I already have knowledge and experience, since I was an accountant in Brazil for over 10 years, and this position was in the accounting department.

Another good point, I was continuing working in the same physical place only indoors, not outdoors anymore; so, I would have the opportunity to continue seeing all of the employees and keep that emotional attachment with them until little by little I got used to it and cut the umbilical cord. I was leaving behind a job that I really enjoyed doing it. Something inside of me was saying that I needed to move forward and do the same for many more people in different areas of their lives, not related to their sales or tips, but in their relationships, prosperity, career, spiritual path, overcoming fears, resentment, guilt, and so on.

Once more I found myself talking to the general manager of the company explaining all my reasons why I wanted to move inside the office even though I knew I was going to make much less money, but I would have freedom to do all the things I desired to do. Money was never my main motivation in life.

The general manager said he was really happy with my performance in the restaurant, so he was not excited about moving me from that position. He thought it was much easier for him to find a secretary than it would be to find a great manager. In one point of view, it was awesome to hear that he is really happy with my job, but on the other hand, I was sad because my great performance was potentially depriving me of the opportunity to go to another position.

As always, I took his response as a yes, and started my affirmations process again. If they had always worked for me before, why wouldn't they work this time when it is for a great reason: To build my business and be able to help many people on their life path.

I started writing over and over affirmations like " I bless my current job with love, and I release it right now for a much better position in the office." I remember I had talked to my boss approximately three times about this opportunity of my moving to the accounting department. One day he came to me and said that he was waiting for one lady to show up and start working, if she did not show up the position was mine.

My intuition was saying that the job was already mine, and I did not have to worry about it anymore. The lady did not present herself at work on the day that she was supposed to. My boss came to me, and said he had been confused about the starting date, she was actually supposed to come the following week. The next week came with no sign of the lady. The general manager told me that he thought it was my lucky day. Luck or not, the job was already mine.

I started working in the office, and had been there about two weeks when the lady that my boss was expecting showed up. So, my boss decided to give it a try and kept us both in the office, except there was not physical space for all of us in there. So, he ended up asking me to work as restaurant manager two days of the week and three days in the office as secretary. In the beginning, it looked like an amazing offer so I had accepted it. But as time went on, I was not happy because I did not want to be working in two different schedules and positions.

I decided to talk to my boss and explain all my frustrations about being in both places. I told him he needed to give me the full-time manager position back or full-time in the office. To make a long story short, for some reason the lady that was hired after me in the office left the company and the position as administrative assistant was mine.

I was really happy, because while I was working in the office, I was able to plug the headphones into my ear and listen to all kinds of interviews related to spiritual, positive changes, affirmations, new techniques so I can keep improving myself and apply into others' lives. Also I had time to attend more workshops, write my first book, study more, get deeper into my self-discovery, give my classes, start my website, be more creative and be open for the many ideas that are coming to my mind.

Recently, I have been listening to my partner talking a lot about ego. Usually when I say something he would always point out to me, "here is your ego talking." But this was happening over and over again until I realized I had to go deeper and find out much more about it. I consider myself a seeker, I like to learn different things and because of the repetition of what he was saying I thought it was a sign for me, or it was something I needed to study about it.

So I decided to start listening to Dr. Wayne Dyer, who talks a lot about ego, about how to die from the ego which is your false self. And, honestly, my mind lately is blowing off in a way that I never expected before. All that happened and is happening in my life is such a blessing and always comes in the right and perfect order.

The bottom line, I am really happy with my life, and I know this is just the beginning of much that is coming. I learned how to see a positive thing even in a bad situation. I found myself more confident, more relaxed, more comprehensive. I learned how to trust my intuition, how to let things go that bother me. I am able to understand that everything happens for a reason.

If I need to get mad or sad with a specific situation that comes into my life, I have time to go over all this anger or sadness, and before long, I am able to let it go and come back to my connection with my source, which I call God. I am happy for finding my purpose in my life, which is to spread the good word and help people achieve their dream life which can be in their spiritual path, or with relationships, career, prosperity, healthy, forgiveness. I am very grateful for this conception of life that is being revealed to the world for the past thirty years, that we can have anything we desire. If we want more love, there is a magic formula to attract more love. If you want prosperity, there is a way for being more prosperous. If we learn all the principles and practice them, they will little by little become a part of your life. The day will come that all the principles will be automatic for you, they will be such a part of your life, you will not even have to think about it. Remember everything in life is practice. If you want to become a singer, you need to practice your voice. If you want to become a good cook, you need to make the dishes over and over again. You might make some mistakes, but they are all part of the process. If you want to be prosperous, you need to learn the principles of how to attract prosperity and practice them again and again until they become a part of you, and then you will start attracting prosperity wherever you are.

NOTHING BETTER TO TALK ABOUT IT THAN LIFE

What does the word "life" mean for you? What kind of feelings do you have when you think about life? Do you have the life you want right now? If you could change your life would you like to do so? Maybe you think life is meant to be suffering? Or perhaps a joyful adventure? Well this depends only and exclusively on you. Anything you experience on your journey, that is your story, that is your life.

If you choose having a fun, fulfilling life, it depends on what you are thinking and believing in order to attract that. If your life is not what you expect, or is not enjoyable, there is something in you that is blocking you from having what you want. Your thoughts and beliefs are not in harmony with what you need to think or believe in order to attract what you want.

If you are not experiencing the reality you want, then there is something in you that you need to change. You can start by paying attention to what you think most of the time and what you believe about any area of your life. If you want to have what you desire, first of all, you need to have the desire to change. Some people want to have a happy and successful life but they do not do anything about it. I know it sometimes take a little while to change, and we keep ourselves resistant, but the first step to take is having the desire to change and then to work on the resistance or procrastination you have to be willing to change.

In the book by Louise Hay, *You Can Heal Your Life*, she talks about the resistance and she talks about the willingness to change and also shares some exercises to work on. I remember when I got stuck while I was working on changes in myself and my thoughts, the first thing I used to do was procrastinate and feel lazy about the change.

So I started practicing this amazing exercise in which I step in front of mirror looking right into my eyes, and I say out loud or sing, "I am willing to change," or "I am willing to release this pattern that no longer serves me."

I started practicing over and over again, repeating anytime I remembered, and I still do today for some things I need to work on. I started feeling changes in my perception, I started becoming more aware in which situations I was resistant or I was procrastinating, and then magically I started feeling the shift. I began changing what it was I needed to change.

Finding which beliefs and thoughts are no longer are serving you, changing these thoughts for positive ones, having the desire to change, working on the resistance and procrastination, being willing to shift, will provide you with all the ingredients to attract what you want. Your consciousness will start feeling the energy that you are sending out to it, and it will begin to transform into the reality that you wish.

Do not concentrate your thoughts on what you do not want, or on what does not work in your life, or what you do not like. If you want to attract more prosperity in your life, but perhaps you always concentrate your thoughts on the lack of money, it is very hard to attract more money. Or maybe you want to be more lovable, but if you usually criticize yourself or think you are not good enough, it will be very difficult to have people that love you in your life. Pay attention to everything that you concentrate on, pay attention, keep talking, thinking, believing in increase in your life.

Our bodies are energy and the vibration we send out to the world is going to come back to us in the same form. For instance, if you like to gossip about others, you are sending a vibration of gossiping, and that is what you are going to attract to your life: people that are going to talk about you or perhaps about your loved ones. Or maybe you always criticize others for their behaviors, basically this means you are sending a message to the Universe and affirming that you want criticism in your life.

Everything that happens outside of ourselves is a reflection of our inner self. Have you heard the expression "what goes around, comes around" or "what we give out, comes back to us"? That is exactly what I am talking about it. If you are experiencing things that you do not want for yourself, it basically means that there is something in you that is attracting that. If you pay attention to your thoughts, beliefs and words you are going to find out why you are pulling these experiences to you.

We have everything inside of us, all the tools to change whatever needs to change. These tools are our thoughts, beliefs, actions, vibration that we put out to the world. We all can do it, if we learn the right way, and if we really want to change.

RELATIONSHIPS ARE OUR MIRRORS

Everyone that surrounds us, including random people or people that are related to us in any form, are mirrors of ourselves. Everything outside of us is a reflection of our inner self. When we meet a certain type of person, this includes our husband, wife, kids, teachers, bosses, co-workers, friends and even random people on the street, it means that there is something in you that is attracting these kinds of people. The people you are attracting to your life are merely people that your inner self is calling to you. These people are there to help us to find where we need to change or heal.

If you meet someone that has something about him or her you do not like, that simply means that there is something in you that is triggering him or her in that specific situation, it is your inner self that is attracting that for you. Is there any time of your life you question yourself, "Why do I attract these people to my life all the time?" Once you find out the real causes or beliefs you have that are pulling these types of people into your life, you will not attract them anymore to your experience because when you become aware of it, you understand why this happens and start working on the healing process.

I believe that everything that happens in our lives is for a reason, and people that we attract into our lives are here to help us in our process of healing and also they are teaching us whatever lessons we might need to learn. Healing yourself and getting rid of the pattern that is calling these types of people to your life is going to take you away from a similar situation in your life, and perhaps the person that you were having the problem with is going to leave your life in an unexpected way just because you no longer have the pattern that was attracting him or her to you. The great thing about all of this is you can see the points you need to change in you, and if you are not able to heal yourself, at least you know what you need to get done and can look for help.

That is why it is so essential and important to have a great relationship with yourself, because that is what you are going to put out into the world and then attract people into the same vibration that you are. When you love yourself, you are going to attract people that are going to love you the way you are. If you criticize yourself, that's exactly what you are going to attract in your life – in other words you are going to meet people or have relationships with people that will criticize you. Even if the person you are attracting to your life does not have a habit of criticizing people, if you are a critical person, you will probably instill in that specific person the criticism.

Acceptance and approval of ourselves is fundamental to attract the right people. If we do not love ourselves, if we do not respect our bodies, then there is something we need to work on. Otherwise we are going to have people in our lives that are not going to love us or respect us.

I had a time in my life I was very needy and could not be alone for even ten minutes. I was always trying to find somebody to go with me somewhere, or I needed to call someone to chat, always attracting the wrong ones to get done whatever was my need. This kept happening until I started working on what was missing and realized that the most important person to be with me is myself.

I can clearly see now that if I want to do something, or if I need to go somewhere, whether it is traveling, shopping, or creating something in my life, the best person to do that is me. If someone wants to join, help and support me, as long as I feel it is appropriate, I am totally fine with that, but if not, that is absolutely awesome anyway. I am not saying that we need to be all by ourselves, never socializing, but what I mean is feeling comfortable with ourselves, accepting the way we are, appreciating our own company, then we are going to attract healthy relationships because it is the message that is coming from inside of us and transforming in our own reality.

It is very important to have an understanding that right now we are in the perfect moment of our lives, and to be sure that out of this situation other better ones are coming. Some doors are closing, but many others are opening. Even in the hard periods of time, there is always a great message or something that is making us more aware, more prepared, stronger. Remember everything happens for a reason, and out of any kind of experience, whether positive or negative, a great lesson is left behind. Let's say, for example, you have a divorce. I understand there is suffering, it is hard, but if you give yourself time, you will find out that the relationship was not the ideal one for you. Or you will find out that person was there with you for a certain period of time of your life where you learned what you needed to, and then it was time to move on. Or maybe that person was attracted by you for a healing process you needed to learn. Or perhaps it was the right person for you to have your healthy and beautiful kids. Only you will know the answer. The only thing you need to do is open your heart and be aware of whatever message comes to you. Sometimes the answer comes in a dream, or it may come when you are walking on the street, or maybe it comes into your mind during a situation that you experienced before. It could come to you in many forms, so just relax and be ready for many awakenings, for they are blessings in your life.

Some people never tap into the awareness because they choose to be in a complaining state of mind or feeling like a victim, and this does not bring any good for our lives. We are just trying to find excuses or someone to blame. But there is only one person responsible for that reality, and that person is us.

When we totally understand that what we attract to our lives is anything we believe or think, there is nobody we can blame. We do not even need to go to the point of feeling guilty, which is not a good feeling, but just be aware of where we made the mistake, work on it, heal ourselves, accept the way it happened and make the changes we need for the next time.

We have a huge desire and tendency to change others. Do not waste your time. Do yourself a favor and change the way you think, the way you act, the things you believe, and you will see miracles happening in your life. Stop finding excuses to change the world.

I had an episode in my life when I was working as a waitress that I had a conflict with a guy that was working as a bartender. For whatever reason, during about 90 percent of his shift, he kept the faucet of the bar running water. For me personally, waste of any kind makes me really sad.

I asked him many, many times to turn off the faucet while he was not using it. His answer most of the time was that I was not the manager in charge, or I was not the person who was paying the bill. I tried to explain to him that it was just a consciousness action related to the environment, that there was not a reason for leaving the faucet open all day long, and I tried over and over to instill some kindness in his heart. I talked to my manager about what was going on, and she talked to him, but for some reason he was not able to get it.

One day we were working together, and again he was getting on my nerves, driving me crazy. For someone to get me in that state, it has to be something that really bothers me. I was ready to punch the guy, but I had the brilliant idea to ask my manager to send me home. Otherwise, I could have lost control and done something that I did not want to do, and I might regret.

When I got home, I was thinking about what I could do to reverse this situation. Leaving my job because of that guy was not the solution. What I needed to do was learn how to handle that type of situation . I knew that if he was acting like that, there was something in me that was triggering him to make me feel that way.

This episode happened on a Monday, and knowing that I would have to work with him again on Thursday, I started designing my plan. I took a piece of paper and started writing over and over again affirmations like " I bless Peter with love, I appreciate him, he closes the faucet every time he finishes using it, he is an adorable bartender, our relationship is harmonious, we work in a happy place, we are surrounded by love," and so on.

Normally, when a situation like that would occur, when I would come back to work, we would not say even hi to each other.   Then little by little we would start talking again. When I went back to work on Thursday, I gave him a big smile, a hug and a kiss. He looked at me so surprised, and asked me what I had done because I was so different that day. I said that it was nothing, I just love my life and life is awesome.

Believe me or not, he was a completely different person behind the bar. I can't say he closed the faucet 100 percent of the time, but I could say 70 percent he did, and I did the other 30 percent even though for me it was extremely difficult to reach the faucet.

After a few months, I moved up to a manager position in another restaurant, and I no longer worked with him. But what I learned from this experience is trying to change someone else is just a waste of your time. If you want to change something or someone, you first need to change the way you feel about or see that person. When you send the good vibration from inside of you, everything outside will respond in the same way. When I was getting mad at him about the faucet, he was answering me in the same vibration, because that is the energy that I was putting out to the world. But when I magically changed the way I saw him and sent him love, appreciation, forgiveness, and compassion, he instantly recognized the change in me and automatically changed his vibration. For me, this was a great lesson, because I was at the point of giving up, quitting, or taking matters into my own hands.

People exist in our lives to push our buttons, to make us see what we need to change in ourselves in order for us to have what we expect in life .

WHAT DOES YOUR BODY FEEL?

Our body is a reflection of what we believe and what we think. In other words, we reflect our inner-self in our bodies. If we experience any condition in our bodies, it means your body is letting you know that there is something you are doing or believing that is not right for you.

I became more aware of my body's messages after I changed my eating habits to vegetarian. I am not trying to say that for you, in order to have a healthier life, you need to become vegetarian. But in my case, I realized that anything you put inside or outside your body, responds to you. The food you eat, the thoughts you have, the way you act, the things you believe. The process of becoming vegetarian came to me in a totally natural way. I have always had the desire to eat healthier. I love vegetables, salads, grains of any kind, nuts, fruits, basically what comes from nature are always welcome, except animals.

Back in Brazil, when I used to practice yoga, I would hear the instructors talk all the time about being vegetarian. I felt they were attempting to force this belief upon me, and as a good "Sagittarian," I don't like anything that is imposed on me. So back then I did not become vegetarian. I guess I was not ready for this change in my life at time, for me it sounded too strict and too imposed.

About two years ago, a friend of mine told me about a naturopath practitioner and suggested that I go to see him. Since then, naturally, without anything being imposed upon me, I became vegetarian. It is amazing how my body responds in a great way, and my mind also is very thankful for that change. I feel much more aware of what is going on with my body and my mind.

If I am feeling some pain, for instance, I know that I might be eating something that is not right for me or maybe the pain is from some beliefs that I need to let go of. I found it a very easy way for me to figure out what action I need to take. I have no idea if I am going to be vegetarian for my whole life, but what I really know is that it feels so good, and I feel inspired more and more to add different ways to be as natural as I can.

Becoming vegetarian is one of the things I found for myself in my awakening process. My mind became more clear, I can think much better. Sometimes it is hard to define, but it really changed my life. I lost the excess weight I had, and my friends say I rejuvenated a lot. I could say that becoming vegetarian, which had seemed impossible to me, taught me that everything is possible, you can overcome anything in your life. I expanded my desire to cook different dishes, adding some different spices and herbs, balancing my diet with the needs that my body has.

It also sparked my interest in natural medicine, which I believe can heal your body using natural herbs, aromatherapy, flower essences, healthy eating habits, also with positive thoughts and releasing all your limitations, resentments, guilt, fear, blame. But again, each one of us has different ways to become more fulfilled and have a healthier life, this was for me a very blessed way.

I believe that we are going to get to the point in our lives that we do not need to see a regular doctor anymore. More and more people around the globe are becoming aware of the causes of their bodies' reactions. We are going to be at a point where we will either be able to cure ourselves or perhaps with the assistance of a naturopathic practitioner.

For me, it is extremely important setting yourself free of all the limitations and beliefs that are holding you from having the life you want, unless you want to have major health problems and be frightened when you are faced with a surgeon's knife. And, if you continue to have the same beliefs or old patterns after a doctor's treatment of an illness, there is an enormous probability of the illness returning.

If you do not change what caused that condition, perhaps you will attract another one in a different area of your body, because illnesses, pain, cuts are just ways that our body finds to tell us that there is something in our minds, in our inner selves, that is not right.

Wayne Dyer showed an experiment in one of his workshops. He called a lady from the audience and asked her to think about a situation in her life when she was really angry, a time that she was in very deep pain, divorce, or someone borrowed a money from her and never paid it back, or someone that abandoned her, or mistreated her, or when she was in a position that she wanted revenge, or wanted to get even with that person.

While she was thinking on that specific time of her life, he pushed down hard on her arm with his hands while he was asking her to resist. What happened when he did this was she did not have any resistance, any force to keep her arm up.

What he showed to the audience was when you feel negatively, think about revenge, or you are in pain, your body gets weak and you do not have the strength that you need. So the bottom line that he wanted to show to all of us is that if you think negatively or use your imagination in a negative way,

Restoring Your Beautiful Life

you start creating a reality of negativity in your body and also in
your world.

ABUNDANCE, PROSPERITY

When I switched my job from the restaurant manager position to
administrative assistant in the accounting department, my salary dropped
a very significant amount. Actually I was advised about that before I even
started working there. In the beginning I was surprised when I received my
very first pay check as assistant, because I was having the thoughts that I
was making less, that I could not handle my bills, that I was already used to
the amount of money I was making before, and the thoughts went on and
on.

I know myself, I usually, at first, take some time to digest the unpleasant
situation that is shown into my life, and then I acknowledge that I need
to get that bad feeling away from me. So in that case, about my salary
going down significantly, I started reconnecting to my source or God in
a very trusting way of which there is never lack, never loss. I made my
affirmations as I always do, such as "I can pay my bills easily, always
on time, money comes to me in unexpected ways, money is my friend,
everything I need is taken care of, no matter what."

The other day my friend asked me how I was doing in paying my rent, car
and all my bills since my salary dropped a lot. I simply answered to her
that the Universe always take care of me, and I do not have to worry about
it. It was my calling to be in the office making less money, since money was
never my main motivation in my life anyway. I've opened my mind to new
things and ideas.

And, believe me, I am handling the situation very well, I am never on top
of how much I have today or tomorrow in my account. I just check when I
need to make a payment, and I trust the money is there, and it really always
is in there.

The situation that you have right now is the result of what you were
thinking yesterday, last week, months, years ago. If you want to change
your situation, today is the right time to do that, so right now start feeling
more prosperous, start affirming that you have abundance of everything
in your life. Close your eyes and imagine abundance coming to you,
everything that is available to you, you just need to learn how to claim it.

A lot of people get depressed about the economy. They want to know what
happened yesterday, and if not satisfied they want to find out what was

going on last week, and they try to figure out what is coming in the future. They are always focusing on the lack of money, what is missing, what they are supposed to be making, and they do not realize that they are getting into this negative world and creating more lack in their lives.

Do not allow yourself to get upset with all these ideas. In times of bad economy there are a lot of opportunities for those who know how to use them. Keeping yourself in the positive vibration, affirm that all you need is always available for you, picture yourself in your mind in abundance of money, love, healthy relationships, happiness, peace. The Universe responds to you in the same vibration that you are sending to It. Feel abundance in your life, and the abundance energy will be attracted by you.

Another way of blocking abundance to ourselves is when we do not feel happy with others' success and prosperity. If we believe that the energy we give out is going to become a reality for us, we should not be jealous or sad because someone is making more money than us, or because someone has a better car than us, or better job. Feeling good about others' situations brings good to us also.

AFFIRMATIONS

Affirmations can be negative or positive statements. They are everything you think and believe. If you think or believe that you are not worthy of relationships, you are simply affirming to the Universe that you do not want loving relationships. If you say or complain about the lack of energy you have, you are saying to the Universe that you want to feel more tired. If you write affirmations about prosperity or act like a prosperous person, you are simply affirming that you want to be more prosperous and that is what you are going to attract. Remember the Universe responds to what we affirm, it does not matter if it is in a positive or negative state.

I remember when I started really getting affirmations in my life, it was hard in the beginning because you start affirming, and then minutes after, you come back to the habitual thinking. But I kept it up, and little by little, I started feeling the shift. Eventually, it became a habit for me.

Take a moment to pay attention to your thoughts or beliefs. Write down all the feelings you have related to money, to your parents, to your family members, co-workers, or what you think about the government, or schools, or people in general, perhaps about your financial situation, about men in general, women, sons, intimacy, and so on. After you write all those down, think where you are holding your negative thinking.

For instance if you believe that men in general are not supportive, change this belief by affirming, " I always attract men into my life that are there for me, they are supportive, they take good care of me."

Or, let's say you think you are not good enough, so you change these thoughts to: "I am good enough, I am creative, ideas come to me easily, and in every way, I love myself."

The most important thing related to affirmations is saying them in the right way. Some people think they are making the affirmations correctly, but in reality they are not. The affirmations first of all have to be positive. Remember to concentrate on what you want.

So let's say you do not like your job and you want to work as a secretary, you start the process of making positive statements related to your new position. You begin affirming, "I love my new job as a secretary, my co-workers are amazing, I work in a respectful environment, I make a great deal of money, my schedule is perfectly awesome, my bosses are very proud of me, I am doing a great job, and I love my new career."

The second important point is the affirmation has to be personal. Of course, you can make affirmations for someone else in the form of sending good vibration, or loving thoughts, prayer, but if someone wants to attract something in his or her life they need to make the affirmations for themselves. We always attract what we are putting the energy on, so if I make an affirmation to another person, but he or she is not affirming what I am, it is not going to work, because the person needs to put intention to it.

The third point of how to make the right affirmation is to make it in the present tense. If you say, I will make very good money, or I will have this car, your affirmation is in the future tense and your dream will always be in the future, the probability to happen what you wish is going to be very low.

Be very precise on what you want, you can add details, colors, taste, texture, size, features, what you want from it, how you want it, be creative about it, use your imagination.

If you make the affirmations respecting each of these three points, you have a huge chance to get what you want. So remember, affirmations have to be positive, personal and in the present tense.

You can make a song with your affirmations, and keep singing it over and over again, or you can say it out loud, or perhaps in front of the mirror looking into your eyes, express gratitude for already receiving what you want, feel like you already have what you wish, smile, act like you already have it.

I would say affirmations really work, but it is very important for you to keep a connection with good feelings about yourself, about others and about life in general so you keep in your field of vibration only good energy, attracting in this way what you want in your life. I believe sometimes things do not happen in exactly the way we want because there must be something you need to learn, a need to get stronger, mature. Life is like a book. We have chapters and into these chapters we have some problems to solve, which I think are not problems but lessons. Once we accept the way it comes into our lives and figure out what we need to adjust in ourselves, we do not have to worry about it. We all are going to be fine.

I remember a while ago, I was making affirmations about a relationship. My affirmations were very rich in details, I was affirming to meet a partner for love. I described the way he treats me, how he looks at me, how he acts related to me and others, I even described his physical features, and also I wanted someone in the spiritual path like me. I was very creative.

So what happened is that not even one month later, I attracted a man into my life. He is exactly what I was looking for, even his physical features. The very best part is that he is very spiritual. We found out later that we both made affirmations before we got to know each other. His affirmations were also asking for someone on spiritual path, and someone who could support and nourish him along his way. We made a connection right away, and we experienced in one month what usually takes people a year.

It was very intense, and at that time I thought I found my soul mate because he was much more than what I was looking for. Later on I realized that the definition of soul mate that I used to have was no longer serving me. I had in my mind, like many others, that a soul mate is the person that is nearly like you in almost everything.

The problems, or I would say the lessons, started coming up in our relationship around two months later. At that time I started questioning myself why in the beginning of the relationship everything looked so perfect, and then later we had so many disagreements. What was wrong with me? I am always in a good mood, I treat others with respect, I have a great energy. I even discussed it with him, but actually nothing changed.

One day I found an interview where Dr. Wayne Dyer talks about soul mate, and then I started understanding much better what was going on. His quote was: "Your Soul mate is the person you cannot stand." He says that when we meet someone and everything looks perfect and neat, we have the tendency of thinking that we truly found our soul mate just because of that. He advises to give yourself one month to see what will happen.

Dr. Dyer explained we have a misunderstanding of what a soul mate is. We think that person will like everything we do, they are going to think the way we think, but that is not exactly what happens. Our soul mate is the person that is attracted to us to push our buttons. And that is exactly what happened to in our relationship.

I started understanding that he came into my life to help me go over things I need to get done. He pushes my bottoms like no one did before, he questioned me a lot, he searches for the truth, he takes me away from my comfort zone many times.

Today I can clearly see that he was sent to me because I asked the Universe for him and because I needed to learn in order to help others to overcome their issues, too. Some relationships do not move forward because people are not able to accept others the way they are, or they are not aware enough to understand that we are in the mode of learning and growing together, or because we spend time together to learn and heal and move on to the next level of learning in our lives.

I also know that he is the bridge for much more awareness to come into my life. I become stronger day by day, I have the ability to see when I commit the mistakes that make him act the way he does. All I can say he is been such a blessing on my path, and I am very grateful for him.

I don't know what life reserves for me next, the only thing I know is I can change my reality and my experiences anytime I want to. Self-discovery is a very exciting journey, and I am delighted to share much more with you so that together we can heal ourselves and the world. Life loves you. Life loves all of us. We are one. Namasté.

TIPS I FOUND USEFUL

FOOD YOU EAT: Eat as much organic "RAW" food as you can. Consume plenty of fresh vegetables, fruits, grains. Avoid packed, canned, industrialized, processed food. Do not use the microwave. Avoid white flour, sugar and especially HIGH FRUCTOSE CORN SYRUP. I recommend that you replace these with royal jelly and/or honey, agave and even Xylitol. All of these recommendations are safe for diabetics as they have low glycemic levels. If you have cravings for sugar you can eat a lot of dry fruits, or smoothies made with fresh fruits.

AROMATHERAPY: Pure essential oils are great medicine, one of the easiest to acquire, safely use, and very effective. It is an amazing way to heal, clean, protect your body and your environment against harmful pathogens.

DRINK "GOOD" WATER: Drink healthy, safe, structured, "living" water. For more information go to the website www.beyondwater.org

EXERCISE REGULARLY: Exercise is good for your body, mind and spirit. Take some time in your day for a walk, yoga, playing sports. Moving your body is going to make you feel much better, it is a great anti-depressant.

PRAYER, MEDITATION, BREATHING: Take time in your day to be in contact with your inner self.

AFFIRMATIONS: Make this a habit from the time you open your eyes in the morning until you close your eyes at night. Think happy thoughts throughout your day.

USE NATURAL PRODUCTS: Avoid as much as possible chemical and synthetic products. Nature is one of the best gifts we have in our lives, use natural and organic products on your body. Your skin is the biggest organ you have, and everything you put on it is going to absorb into your system right away.

TAKE GOOD CARE OF NATURE: Recycle as much as possible, avoid using disposable items that harm the environment, save energy and water. Teach our children and future generations how to do their part to preserve the planet. Treat the animal and plant kingdoms with respect and care. It is so important that we take immediate action related to our Mother Earth and begin repairing the damage that has been done.

IN CASE IF YOU GET AN ILLNESS OF ANY KIND: Look for a natural cure and/or treatment. Nature has an enormous range of vitamins, minerals, herbs that can take very good care of you and your loved one's health. Or simply eat "RAW" fruits and vegetables as much as possible.

ABOUT THE AUTHORS

NANCY NEWMAN

Nancy Newman, the Holistic Mind-Body-Spirit Personal RE-formation©
expert, is a writer, editor, teacher, internationally-known speaker, and
licensed Heal Your Life® Coach/Workshop Facilitator with a private
practice, Mindful Wellness, in Spokane, Washington. Her latest book is
Beyond Beautiful.

Nancy is also a certified Reiki Master, Reflexologist, and registered Master
Toe Reader. She enjoys traveling to Portland, Oregon to spend time with
her son, daughter-in-law and new grandbaby, London Ava.

www.yourmindfulwellness.com
nancy@yourmindfulwellness.com

LISA A. HARDWICK

Lisa A. Hardwick is an expert in holistic inner child healing, a licensed Heal Your Life® teacher, author, speaker, workshop leader and a board member for her local chapter Children's Advocacy Center in East Central Illinois.

She resides in Charleston, Illinois, where she enjoys spending time with her three adult sons, her family and friends. She also enjoys traveling throughout the world, sharing her testimony and assisting others on their path to an authentic and beautiful life.

Lisa assists others in sharing their own stories and important messages of healing, hope and love. Through her author services company, she guides her clients in the transition from aspiring writers to published authors. Lisa and her company are passionate about providing a unique, personal, hands-on approach at each step of the way, from creating the message out of the initial idea stage to editing, layout, printing, and marketing. Lisa and her company are dedicated to assist you to produce and publish your book! For more information, contact lisa@lisahardwick.com .

www.lisahardwick.com
lisa@lisahardwick.com

MELISSA J. WHITE

Melissa J. White is a writer, speaker, teacher and life coach who empowers people nationwide to live more authentic lives. She is passionate about living her truth and assisting others in accessing their inner wisdom.

Melissa earned her undergraduate degree in counseling from Marshall University, her graduate degree in higher education from Ball State University, and her law degree from The American University, Washington College of Law. She is a certified Radical Forgiveness Coach and Workshop Facilitator and a Registered Yoga Teacher.

Born and raised in West Virginia, Melissa has lived throughout the United States. She is currently living on the west coast.

www.mylifeopportunities.com
melissa@mylifeopportunities.com

TERRY VOLIN REAM

Terry Volin Ream is a licensed Heal Your Life® Coach, Spiritual Life Coach and Facilitator of workshops which inspire life-changing experiences for individuals who want to create the life they really want.

She empowers you to be more true to yourself and awaken to life, hope, love and happiness.

www.AllisWell4you.com
Terry.Ream@yahoo.com

TAMMY GYNELL LAGOSKI

Tammy Gynell Lagoski is a published author, publishing consultant, knowledgeable in Grief Coaching and working with diverse populations. She was raised on a farm in Charleston, Illinois and currently resides in Peoria, Illinois, where she enjoys spending time with her husband, daughter, three step daughters, sons-in-law and new grand baby. She also enjoys spending time with her two dogs, Frankie and Molly, who are as rambunctious as a couple of two year olds.

www.tammylagoski.com
tammylag@gmail.com

MOLLY WELESKI

Molly Weleski lived in demoralizing depression and a haze of antidepressants until she stumbled upon the teachings of Louise L Hay through her book, *You Can Heal Your Life*. This book taught her how working on the principles of self love, forgiveness, anger and guilt would bring her to a place of joy that she would have never imagined. Inspired and passionate about revealing what she has found, Molly dedicates her life to assisting people in their personal growth and spiritual awareness through her Workshops and Life Coaching.

Molly is an impassioned speaker and teacher with the ability to inspire life-changing growth. She now works with the natural laws of the universe and is certain that we are what we believe ourselves to be; our thoughts create our lives. Molly is committed to living consciously, honoring all parts of her Self and trusting her Self. Her current expression of joy, abundance and healthy relationships are living proof of an internal transformation making change in the outside world. Molly delights in laughter and has a love for life that translates into her ability to touch others and guide them in their own amazing transformations.

www.mollyweleski.com
molly@mollyweleski.com

KIMBERLY S. PRATTE

Kimberly S. Pratte is a published author born in Cincinnati, and raised in Illinois. As an adult she has lived in many places, including Washington State, California, Georgia, Tennessee, and overseas in Germany.

Now living in Milwaukee, Wisconsin, Kimberly is a student at the School of Integrative Psychology, and works full-time for an Executive Search Firm. She enjoys spending time with her four wonderful children, two grandchildren, and friends.

www.kimberlypratte.com
kimpratte@gmail.com

SHELLY YORK

Shelly York is a licensed Heal Your Life ® workshop leader, a writer and a self-described Promoter of Happiness. She specializes in educating others in self-love while speaking from the heart and sharing her own personal experiences.

Shelly lives in Southern California with her beautiful daughter, Madison. She finds her joy in the simple things in life and believes that daily visits to Starbucks are an absolute must!

www.shellyyork.com
Shellyyork@rocketmail.com

JODY KRATZ

Jody Kratz RN, BSN has worked in the healing profession for decades and is a certified, insured, and licensed Heal Your Life® Instructor and Life Coach. She has also trained personally with Sonia Choquette and is a certified sixth sensory practitioner.

Jody realized early on in her nursing career that there was a strong mind, body, spirit connection. Unfortunately, western medicine is focused on the body and disease. She has witnessed firsthand the effects that both negative and positive thoughts can have on a person's health and entire life. You can change your life by changing your negative thoughts and beliefs. This is what drew her to the work of Louise Hay and led her to become a *Heal Your Life®* teacher and life coach. She loves teaching workshops and witnessing the joy people experience when they realize they truly can create the life they have always wanted. There is nothing more satisfying to Jody than to work one-on-one with a coaching client and see the amazing growth and change they experience over time.

Jody studied metaphysics to help overcome many difficulties and a few tragedies in her personal life. She has studied the works of some of the world's most prominent teachers such as Marianne Williamson, Caroline Myss, Wayne Dyer, Abraham, Eckhart Tolle, and several others. Jody takes all that she has learned over the years and incorporates it into her workshops and coaching programs. She is confident that she can save you several years of searching and trial and error to create the life you always dreamed of having. Her workshops and coaching programs can get you on the fast track to creating your own dream life. Are you ready to invest in yourself and your own inner talents to create the life of your dreams? If the answer is yes, you have come to the right place.

www.innerlifeinvestments.com
jody@innerlifeinvestments.com

CAROL ROESE

Carol Roese is a speaker, writer and life change coach.

Carol is originally from Brazil and has been in the U.S. for nine years. She currently lives in Miami, FL. Her passion is to inspire and motivate people to live a happier, healthier and fuller lives.

She shares her amazing stories, passions and ideas in a pleasant Brazilian way through her character and Brazilian accent. She truly believes that if each one of us do something positive for others and themselves , we can all share a peaceful, abundant and joyful world together.

www.Awake2Change.com
carol@awake2change.com
786-266-8136

RESOURCES

The following list of resources are for the national headquarters; search in your yellow pages under "Community Services" for your local resource agencies and support groups.

AIDS

CDC National AIDS Hotline
(800) 342-2437

ALCOHOL ABUSE

Al-Anon Family Group Headquarters
1600 Corporate Landing Parkway
Virginia Beach, VA 23454-5617
(888) 4AL-ANON
www.al-anon.alateen.org

Alcoholics Anonymous (AA)
General Service Office
475 Riverside Dr., 11th Floor
New York, NY 10115
(212) 870-3400
www.alcoholics-anonymous.org

Children of Alcoholics Foundation
164 W. 74th Street
New York, NY 10023
(800) 359-COAF
www.coaf.org

Mothers Against Drunk Driving
MADD
P.O. Box 541688
Dallas, TX 75354
(800) GET-MADD
www.madd.org

National Association of Children of
Alcoholics (NACoA)
11426 Rockville Pike, #100
Rockville, MD 20852
(888) 554-2627
www.nacoa.net
Women for Sobriety
P.O. Box 618
Quartertown, PA 18951
(215) 536-8026
www.womenforsobriety.org

CHILDREN'S RESOURCES

Child Molestation
Childhelp USA/Child Abuse Hotline
15757 N. 78th St.
Scottsdale, AZ 85260
(800) 422-4453
www.childhelpusa.org

Prevent Child Abuse America
200 South Michigan Avenue, 17th Floor
Chicago, IL 60604
(312) 663-3520
www.preventchildabuse.org

Crisis Intervention
Girls and Boys Town National Hotline
(800) 448-3000
www.boystown.org

Children's Advocacy Center of East Central Illinois
(If your heart feels directed to make a donation to this center,
please include Lisa Hardwick's name in the memo – she would be most grateful)
616 6th Street
Charleston, IL 61920
(217) 345-8250
http://caceci.org

Children of the Night
14530 Sylvan St.
Van Nuys, CA 91411
(800) 551-1300
www.childrenofthenight.org

Covenant House Hotline
(800) 999-9999
www.covenanthouse.org

National Children's Advocacy Center
210 Pratt Avenue
Huntsville, AL 35801
(256) 533-KIDS (5437)
www.nationalcac.org

CO-DEPENDENCY

Co-Dependents Anonymous
P.O. Box 33577
Phoenix, AZ 85067
(602) 277-7991
www.codependents.org

SUICIDE, DEATH, GRIEF

AARP Grief and Loss Programs
(800) 424-3410
www.aarp.org/griefandloss

Grief Recovery Institute
P.O. Box 6061-382
Sherman Oaks, CA 91413
(818) 907-9600
www.grief-recovery.com

Suicide Awareness Voices of Education
(SAVE)
Minneapolis, MN 55424
(952) 946-7998

Suicide National Hotline
(800) 784-2433

DOMESTIC VIOLENCE

National Coalition Against Domestic
Violence
P.O. Box 18749
Denver, CO 80218
(303) 831-9251
www.ncadv.org

National Domestic Violence Hotline
P.O. Box 161810
Austin, TX 78716
(800) 799-SAFE
www.ndvh.org

DRUG ABUSE

Cocaine Anonymous National Referral
Line
(800) 347-8998

National Helpline of Phoenix House
(800) COCAINE
www.drughelp.org

National Institute of Drug Abuse
(NIDA)
6001 Executive Blvd., Room 5213,
Bethesda, MD 20892-9561, Parklawn
Building
Info: (301) 443-6245
Help: (800) 662-4357
www.nida.nih.gov

EATING DISORDER

Overeaters Anonymous
National Office
P.O. Box 44020
Rio Rancho, NM 87174-4020
(505) 891-2664
www.overeatersanonymous.org

GAMBLING

Gamblers Anonymous
International Service Office
P.O. Box 17173
Los Angeles, CA 90017
(213) 386-8789
www.gamblersanonymous.org

HEALTH ISSUES

American Chronic Pain Association
P.O. Box 850
Rocklin, CA 95677
(916) 632-0922
www.theacpa.org

American Holistic Health Association
P.O. Box 17400
Anaheim, CA 92817
(714) 779-6152
www.ahha.org

The Chopra Center at
La Costa Resort and Spa
Deepak Chopra, M.D.
2013 Costa Del Mar
Carlsbad, CA 92009
(760) 494-1600
www.chopra.com

The Mind-Body Medical Institute
110 Francis St., Ste. 1A
Boston, MA 02215
(617) 632-9530 Ext. 1
www.mbmi.org

National Health Information Center
P.O. Box 1133
Washington, DC 20013-1133
(800) 336-4797
www.health.gov/NHIC

Preventive Medicine Research
Institute
Dean Ornish, M.D.
900 Brideway, Ste 2
Sausalito, CA 94965
(415) 332-2525
www.pmri.org

MENTAL HEALTH

American Psychiatric Association of America
1400 K St. NW
Washington, DC 20005
(888) 357-7924
www.psych.org

Anxiety Disorders Association of America
11900 Parklawn Dr., Ste. 100
Rockville, MD 20852
(310) 231-9350
www.adaa.org

The Help Center of the American Psychological Association
(800) 964-2000
www.helping.apa.org

National Center for Post Traumatic Stress Disorder
(802) 296-5132
www.ncptsd.org
National Alliance for the Mentally Ill
2107 Wilson Blvd., Ste. 300
Arlington, VA 22201
(800) 950-6264
www.nami.org

National Depressive and Manic-Depressive Association
730 N. Franklin St., Ste. 501
Chicago, IL 60610
(800) 826-3632
www.ndmda.org

National Institute of Mental Health
6001 Executive Blvd.
Room 81884, MSC 9663
Bethesda, MD 20892
(301) 443-4513
www.nimh.nih.gov

SEX ISSUES

Rape, Abuse and Incest
National Network
(800) 656-4673
www.rainn.org

National Council on Sexual Addiction
and Compulsivity
P.O. Box 725544
Atlanta, GA 31139
(770) 541-9912
www.ncsac.org

SMOKING

Nicotine Anonymous World Services
419 Main St., PMB #370
Huntington Beach, CA 92648
(415) 750-0328
www.nicotine-anonymous.org

STRESS ISSUES

The Biofeedback & Psychophysiology
Clinic
The Menninger Clinic
P.O. Box 829
Topeka, KS 66601-0829
(800) 351-9058
www.menninger.edu

New York Open Center
83 Spring St.
New York, NY 10012
(212) 219-2527
www.opencenter.org

The Stress Reduction Clinic Center for
Mindfulness
University of Massachusetts
Medical Center
55 Lake Ave., North
Worcester, MA 01655
(508) 856-2656

TEEN

Al-Anon/Alateen
1600 Corporate Landing Parkway
Virginia Beach, VA 23454-5617
(888) 425-2666
www.al-anon.alateen.org

Planned Parenthood
810 Seventh Ave.
New York, NY 10019
(800) 230-PLAN
www.plannedparenthood.org

Hotlines for Teenagers
Girls and Boys Town National Hotline
(800) 448-3000

Childhelp National Child Abuse Hotline
(800) 422-4453

Just for Kids Hotline
(888) 594-KIDS

National Child Abuse Hotline
(800) 792-5200

National Runaway Hotline
(800) 621-4000

National Youth Crisis Hotline
(800)-HIT-HOME

Suicide Prevention Hotline
(800) 827-7571

BIBLIOGRAPHY

Canfield, Jack (2005).
>The Success Principles: How to Get from Where You Are to Where You Want to Be.
>New York, NY: Collins

Choquette, Sonia.
>The Answer Is Simple… Love yourself, Live your Spirit
>Hay House

Cohen, Alan.
>"Create A Masterpiece; When mistakes turn into miracles."
>healyourlife.com. N.p., 31 Dec. 2010. Web. 13 Mar. 2011.

Crane, Patricia J. (2002.)
>Ordering From the Cosmic Kitchen:
>The Essential Guide to Powerful, Nourishing Affirmations. Bonsall, CA.
The Crane's Nest.

Hay, Louise L.
>(1982.) Heal Your Body. Carlsbad, CA. Hay House, Inc.
>(1984.) You Can Heal Your Life. Carlsbad, CA. Hay House, Inc.
>(2002.) You Can Heal Your Life Companion Book. Carlsbad, CA. Hay House, Inc.
>(1991.) The Power Is Within You. Carlsbad, CA. Hay House, Inc.

"Inspirational Quotations by Alan Cohen."
>alancohen.com. N.p., n.d. Web. 13 Mar. 2011.

Lesser, Elizabeth.
>Broken Open.
>N.p.: Random House, 2005. Print

Lipton, Bruce H., Ph.D. (2005.)
>The Biology of Belief: Unleashing the Power of Consciousness,
>Matter & Miracles. Carlsbad, CA.
>Hay House, Inc.

Millman, Dan.
>The Life You Were Born To Live. Tiburon, CA:
>HJ Kramer Inc, 1993. Print.

Ruiz , Don Miguel.
>The Four Agreements
>Amber-Allen Publishing

Time, Space, Miracles, and Belief. Carlsbad, CA.
>Hay House, Inc.

Tolle, Eckhart. (1999.)
>The Power of Now: A Guide to Spiritual Enlightenment.
>Novato, CA. New World Library.
>A New Earth: awakening to Your Life's Purpose.
>N.p.: Plume, 2008. Print.

Williamson, Marianne. (2009).
>The Age of Miracles: Embracing the New Midlife.
>Carlsbad, CA. Hay House

DEDICATIONS AND ACKNOWLEDGMENTS

Melissa J. White

I am blessed with an abundance of amazing friends and family who have each played a unique role in my journey. The paths that we have walked and the resulting experiences that we shared have made me who I am today. With some, I have shared a lifetime; with others, some very special moments in time. Some have loved and nurtured me with unconditional support and others have loved me in ways that broke my heart open. It is with much love and profound gratitude that I dedicate this book to each of these people, who have enabled me to create a life worth living.

For providing me with a framework for my journey, I give my heartfelt thanks to: J.R. Keener for teaching me how to listen to and trust in my inner wisdom; Rishi Maha Mandaleshwar Sri Shambhavananda for creating a beautiful yoga retreat and continuing a yogic tradition and meditation practice that sustains me; and Colin Tipping for providing me with a new paradigm through which to cultivate forgiveness.

For making this project a reality, I am deeply grateful to: Lisa A. Hardwick and Robyn Podboy for presenting me with the opportunity to share my story; Vincent Harris for providing ongoing support and advice throughout the process; and my grandmother, Virginia Wheatley White, who taught me and inspired me to write.

Terry Ream

I have been inspired by so many wonderful authors and teachers that transformed my thinking and enabled me to move into the land of conscious living. It is a challenge to name them all.

I am most grateful for my family and friends whose prayers gave me the energy to heal and continue living a life with purpose. A warm, and loving thank you to Nancy Cline, my good friend, who guided me from heaven. A heartfelt thank you goes to my sister, Mary Volin, who gave me the confidence to write.

Most of all thank you "Dad" for teaching me the power of kindness in everyday living.

Tammy G. Lagoski

My chapter is dedicated to my husband who has believed in me and accepted me for the woman I am; as well as my daughter, who is my special gift from God.

If it weren't for my Psychology professors at McKendree University, I would never have been able to write...thank you: Dr. Hoffman, Dr. Kemp and Dr. Bosse.

Thank you to Lisa A. Hardwick for believing in me and encouraging me to believe in my dreams and the rest of the authors of this book for their undying friendship and respect.

Molly Weleski

My chapter is dedicated to my husband, Kim, son, Dustin, and daughter, Jaisy Dai, for their unconditional love, enduring support and their gifted sense of humor.

Special Thanks to Lisa A Hardwick for her beautiful heart and her inspiring soul.

Kimberly Pratte

I dedicate my chapter to my children, my family, my friends, and especially Kris. Thank you for your support and unconditional love through it all. I am truly blessed.

My writing is in response to my life experiences, my desire is to help others along their journey of healing and self-discovery.

I have the privilege of knowing and working with Jim Morningstar, Founder and Director of Transformations Incorporated, the School of Integrative Psychology, and InWellness. Jim's integrative approach to healing your whole body ~ Mind, Body and Spirit ~ has truly transformed my life.

Thank you to Lisa A. Hardwick and Vincent Harris for providing the opportunity and inspiration to be a part of this incredible journey.

Shelly York

My chapter is dedicated in loving memory of my Dad, Paul Raymond Crane. Thank you, Dad, for giving me my wings to fly.

It is through the love, encouragement and support of my Mom, my ex-husband, Mike, and my precious daughter, Madison, that I have been able to pursue my dreams. Unknowingly to my Mom, she introduced me at a very early age to the power of affirmations and for that I will forever be grateful. Thank you Mike for being a part of my life and helping to shape me into the person that I am today! My beautiful daughter Madison is my absolute reason for being ~ need I say more?!

Shortly after meeting Lisa Hardwick, I told her that I just knew that she was going to be a "driving force" in my life. I was right! Thank you Lisa for the opportunity to share my "truth."

Jody Kratz

Never regret having chosen or met Wrong People in our life, because NO ONE can teach us right lessons better than Wrong People. ~ Tathaastu

My chapter is dedicated to the "teachers" that helped me learn the lessons in life that I needed to create my beautiful new life. Special eternal gratitude to my mother, Joanne Shearman, who has always loved and believed in me when no one else did. She is my rock.

Carol Roese

This book is dedicated in memory to my dad, Carlos Alberto Roese. Thank you Dad, for all your love and unforgettable humor. It is also dedicated to my mom, Neusa Roese, for her courage and wisdom.

I acknowledge all who assisted me with growth and becoming who I am, especially to Louise Hay for inspiring me to heal myself and sparking my interest to become a stepping stone for others on their own journey to wellness.

Lastly, a special mention to Lisa Hardwick for directing me on the path that led to making my dream come true of writing my first book.

Nancy Newman

It was my honor to share the journeys of the women in this book and to assist each of them in bringing their stories to the world. I am confident that any reader will be able to find a part of his or her own unique story in one or more of the stories in this book. The life experiences of each of these women will inspire the reader to believe that change is not only possible, but can be achieved!

I am grateful to all the teachers and mentors in my life, including my family who were my greatest teachers, although at times I didn't realize it! I am especially grateful to my son, Dan, his wife, Jenni, and their daughter, London Ava, who lights the path of all who come in contact with her, for their unconditional love. I am particularly grateful for the presence in my life of my best friend, Mavis, who continually reminds me that it is okay to be your authentic self, and that all things are possible.

I am also grateful to Lisa Hardwick for her friendship, love, and consistently positive attitude! She is a bright light who is bringing hope, help and healing to the planet.

Lisa Hardwick

I am abundantly grateful for each and every one of these amazing women. Each shared their own "truths" while incorporating inspiring messages to assist readers on their own personal journey to wellness. They have each removed their own masks and shared their beaming light which in turn allows others to remove barriers and shine their beautiful light as well.

I would further like to take this opportunity to acknowledge Nancy Newman. Nancy is an amazing woman who gives of her talents effortlessly. Without her, this book would have not come to be in its present form. Thank you Nancy – for sharing yourself with us, for your amazing heart and all that you are.

LOOKING FOR CONTRIBUTING AUTHORS!!

Most people have a story that needs to be shared – could YOU be one of the contributing authors we are seeking to feature in one of our upcoming books?

Whether you envision yourself participating in an inspiring book with other authors, or whether you have a dream of writing your very own book, we may be the answer *YOU* have been searching for!!

Are you interested in learning how sharing your message will assist with building your business network, which in turn will result in being able to assist even more people?

Our commitment is to make this planet we call "home" a better place. One of the ways we fulfill our commitment is assisting others in sharing their inspiring messages.

We are looking forward to working with you. To see if this might be the opportunity for YOU, email Lisa Hardwick at lisa@lisahardwick.com.

www.ingramcontent.com/pod-product-compliance
Lightning Source LLC
Chambersburg PA
CBHW031256090426
42742CB00007B/478